Enlightenment

Looking Back to Move Forward

Debra A. K. Thompson

ISBN: 978-0692859582

Published by Candy Publishing, LLC
www.candypublishing.net

Printed in the United States of America

Cover Design, DK1 Promotions

Editor, Lara McKnight

Debra A. K. Thompson

DEDICATION

This book is dedicated to my favorite husband. I am not sure if you knew what you signed up for when you said "I do" almost 40 years ago. Somehow, through it all, you have managed to stick with me through thick and thin, high and low, plenty and want to give me the kind of life any woman would be proud to live. Thank you for your encouragement, caution, support, and more because it has propelled me to do things I might not have ordinarily done. I love you and there's nothing you can do about it.

I also dedicate this book to my three sons, who have been the inspiration for many of the things I have done in my life. Without you guys I would not be the woman or the mother I am today. I thank God every day He loaned you all to me, and I hope I have done Him justly in the way I contributed to your raising.

CONTENTS

FOREWORD

During the lifetime of an individual, situations and problems are encountered in which it is believed that the natural solution is very clear. This conclusion is definitely not arrived at through any position of arrogance, but through naiveté. Sometimes in our lives, God must relegate us to a position of learning in order for a lesson to be taught. When similar circumstances continue to occur in our lives, often our thinking is being challenged. Only then can we fully appreciate the complexity of the situation that helps to expand our thinking. This is what is known as a moment of enlightenment.

This book explores situations of this nature and ponders the broader implications of solutions viewed from different perspectives. Negotiation and compromise must be considered in all situations if a just and valid solution is the ultimate aim. In the uncertainties we face throughout life, it is necessary to expand our horizons and consider a variety of alternatives. This book invites the reader to consider the expanded view of tolerance for varied viewpoints, unusual circumstances, and strange arguments in the approach to any permanent solution. It must always be understood and in the forefront of our minds that "Our ways are not God's ways." This viewpoint is worthy of constant consideration and further examination before drawing any conclusions.

The eternal appeal of this book is, therefore, for a deeper understanding of the other path, the other way, the other view to any situation or problem. The author expresses a viewpoint that is based on information grounded in experiences that are valuable to many people. That's why this book is well worth reading because it has tremendous significance and personal benefit to anyone who embarks on a broader view of their social reality.

Dr. Gerald F. Whittaker

ENLIGHTENMENT

Looking Back To Move Forward

PREFACE

This book is not the book I originally intended to write, but through the process of self-examination, introspection, and thought, I realized these stories had to be told and shared in a more succinct way. The facts surrounding each story are true, but many of the names have been changed to provide continuity and substance to each character. The basis of this book is not to necessarily explore the lives of each character; on the contrary, it is to relay the lessons that Taffnee Johnson has learned through her interactions with these people. Learning is a continuous process, and our job is to try and learn each lesson as quickly as we can. Some lessons are easy to understand and we catch on immediately. Other lessons, however, take a long time to process, digest, and apply. It all depends on your willingness to learn.

It seems that every book you write and every story you tell encompasses some part of you in the final analysis. That is probably why more people fail to tell their story because it takes a lot of time and energy to delve into the real meaning of a situation without revealing some part of who you are. Most of us consider ourselves "private people," making it very difficult to reveal inner thoughts and feelings without revealing the real you.

Everyone wants to be well-thought-of by others, so we constantly adjust and readjust ourselves to fit into the persona we have created. However, God in His infinite wisdom has made each of us as unique characters on a journey unlike that of anyone else's journey. Although we may share the same time and space continuum with others, the lessons we learn from our experiences are uniquely designed for us alone. No one can learn the lessons for us, but the learning can be made easier if our minds are open and receptive.

Self-experience is one way we can begin to learn life lessons. "Self-experience" means exactly what it says - learning everything on your own, through your own experiences which encompass the good, the bad, and the ugly. Some experiences are good to learn on your own, but you must be willing to take the good with the bad if you are unwilling to learn any other way.

Another way to learn a lesson is through reading and education. This means we place ourselves in position to study the experiences and knowledge of others in order to learn life lessons. However, you must be willing to get out and make practical application of the book knowledge you have learned; otherwise, you have learned nothing at all.

A third way to learn a lesson is to learn from the experiences of others. This method implies learning by watching the lives of others and following their example. Patterning your life after another may be good and may save you a lot of heartache and pain in the long run, but you must make sure it is the example you really want to follow. Sometimes things look one way on the outside, but when you peel back the layers surrounding life it is not always what it seems.

Most of us take aspects of each theory to help us learn our life lessons. We can tell others about our lessons, but the real learning has to be experienced by the individual or it means nothing. There is no right or wrong way to learn, but learning can be made easier or more difficult depending on which route you take.

Have you ever heard a joke and when the punch line was finally reached, you didn't get it? Although the person may have told the joke well, and some people may be laughing hysterically, others are sitting with a blank look on their face wondering what was so funny. However, as you think about the joke and the punch line, all of a sudden the light comes on and you begin to laugh. It may have taken a few moments, or it may have taken a few hours, but ultimately you get the point. There are many theories that can explain this phenomenon, but Oprah Winfrey says it best when she calls it an "Ah Ha moment." It's the moment when the light finally comes on and you truly understand what it's all about.

I have found moments of enlightenment happen when the light finally comes on in your thinking and you perceive the significance of some earlier event that you could not understand at the time it happened. The earlier event did not make sense to you, nor could you put the incident into perspective at the time. You were never sure what you did to make such a thing happen, and you were never sure if you could have prevented it from happening. But when illumination finally comes, it becomes abundantly clear what it was all about and what you needed to learn. Some of these moments are connected to major life lessons while others are just things that happen that help you learn and mature as a result.

All of us as human beings have experiences in our lives that surprise us, shock us, devastate us, and enlighten us as we journey through life. Many of these experiences are things that happen just as a matter of course and they are supposed to occur. Other circumstances impact us as a result of unwise decisions, choices, or happenstance. Such events may include: births, deaths, growth, love, or sorrow. We are all familiar with these situations, but the combination of these occurrences mixed with our upbringing, family structure, values and destiny will have a profound impact on how these experiences will ultimately shape our lives.

Although I know I am not the only one who has had these moments of enlightenment, I wanted to share the lessons I've learned with others. Consequently, I have taken the time to organize the most pronounced lessons to share with those who will receive them. This is also an opportunity for others to think about their own life experiences and understand them in the context of an enlightenment moment. Again, these are my true life lessons that may help others put some meaning and purpose to their own experiences.

Like most people, I have had many joys, sorrows, pleasures, and pains that I did not always understand. Sometimes I received blessings I felt I really did not deserve. Other times, I received disappointments I did not expect. There were experiences I went through that had no real significant meaning at the time, but were a part of the growth and development stages of my life. However, I now realize there were experiences that I went through that played a major role in the shaping of my personality, character, and thought processes for my accomplishments later on in life.

Every part of my story is true to the best of my recollection; however, the names have been changed to provide continuity without embarrassment. I wanted to tell my story in such a way as to relate the important lessons I learned without focusing on any particular individual. Many of the people who have crossed my life's path are people I may have known well. Others were not as well-known to me, but their role in my life, however brief, had an impact. Although I may not fully remember everyone's names, their contributions to my growth and development were significant enough to re-tell the story. It is not that they were not important to me, but their names have escaped me as the years have gone by. Moreover, their names are not as important as the actual event I wanted to highlight and the lessons I have learned through them.

Each story is organized in periods of time that I am calling "parts." for the purpose of separating each enlightenment period. Some lessons are funny as I recount them and some lessons are more serious. It has taken me many years to understand the things I now understand. This does not mean I know everything, but it helps me to find the real value in the things I have experienced and treasure those things that are important.

I have found that there are those who may not learn their life lessons right away, but when the light finally appears, it will be easier to recognize it for what it is. Many will not recognize or accept the significance right away, but time has a way of bringing the lessons back around until they are learned. I have found that people who feel they are in a vicious cycle probably haven't learned the real lesson; therefore, they remain in a stagnant state never understanding why they have not moved further in their development. A true defining moment must happen if the real destiny is to ever be fulfilled.

I have chosen to share a few of these moments from my own life lessons that I feel are significant and have had a profound impact on who and what I have become. The things I am sharing are not all inclusive, but represent snapshots in time worthy of further analysis. We all have significant things that happen to us, but there are only a few defining moments that truly bring enlightenment into your life. The ones I have written about are the ones I feel are the most significant and have brought about the most illumination for me.

This is my attempt to tell my story through the character of Taffnee Johnson. Taffnee is not unlike many other young African-American girls raised in the South during the 60's and 70's. She came from a lower-middle-class family in a predominantly Black community where she was nurtured and protected from many of the pitfalls of life. She was raised with both her father and mother in the home and a very tight nuclear family structure.
She has touched the lives of many people, but she has also been touched by the lives of others she has come to know. Take this journey with her and see where it goes.

PART I

Friendship, Discrimination & Forgiveness

My name is Taffnee. The year was 1967 and I was an enthusiastic, but green, junior high school student. Excitement about finally being in junior high school meant that I was growing up and could now do some things I had not been able to do as an elementary school student. This meant I could go to football games, basketball games, and track meets – and maybe even become a cheerleader or majorette. I also realized I would be meeting more mature guys, not just the regular neighborhood guys. I was full of hope and anticipation at the prospect of expanding my newly-found wings in ways that I didn't think possible during my elementary school years. Another noticeable difference between elementary school and junior high school was the fact that we had far more White children attending our school. This was a totally different experience from the elementary school I attended, where the majority of students were Black.

There were only two junior high schools designated for Black children to attend during those days: Sixteenth Street Junior High School and the one I attended, Southside Junior High School. Southside Junior High School like Sixteen Street was located in the middle of a predominantly Black community. The majority of the White kids had to be bused into the school, while most of the Black students walked to school. My neighborhood was one of those communities considered close enough to walk.

Once I started attending Southside, I found it to be a great school, filled with other excited teens and pre-teens like me. I always considered myself very friendly and outgoing, but I wanted to make more friends. I already had several good friends who lived in the neighborhood, but I wanted to get to know more children outside of my community. I made it my business to try and meet as many kids as I possibly could, regardless of their race. I woke up each morning excited about what the next day would bring as I journeyed off to school, anticipating some new adventure to absorb.

I made a lot of new friends during my first semester of school, but the first non-Black guy I met was Jack Mahoney – a very handsome, tall, lanky White guy with blonde hair and blue eyes. Jack was in the 9th grade, but he was very friendly and outgoing just like me. Although I was just a 7th grader, he and I hit it off right away. We would see each other in the mornings before school started and talk and laugh about all kinds of silly things. Most of the other White children rode the school bus to school, but Jack was driven to school by his mom each morning. He told me she had to be at work early, so it was more convenient for her to drop him off. Therefore, I would always arrive at school a little early just so we would have time to talk before classes started. We would always meet at the front of the school because it wasn't over-crowded with students and we could talk without a lot of interruption from other people.

There were also several other kids who met us at the front of the school and we would all engage in playful conversation and fun activities. One of those people who joined us each morning was Susan Martinez. Susan was Jack's girlfriend. They seemed to be a nice couple and I liked both of them very much. Susan was in the 9th grade just like Jack. She was a very pretty girl who had very dark hair and very dark eyes. By all standards I think she was considered very attractive.

I also had another friend by the name of Kim James who met us as well. Kim was a beautiful dark brown girl with a Barbie-doll figure. She got dropped off at school by her boyfriend on most mornings and I enjoyed talking to her also. There were a number of other kids I liked to hang around, but these were the ones I liked to talk to the most before school started.

There were always a few other kids who would gather in front of the school, sitting on the steps or standing around on the sidewalk in small groups laughing and talking; consequently, that's how I got a chance to know so many people. Since I got along so well with Jack and Susan, I felt comfortable venturing out to make more White friends who were in my same grade and classes, and who I thought would be equally as much fun to know.

In my homeroom there was a mixture of White and Black kids. Some of them I knew from the neighborhood, but many of them were children I did not know. There was one girl in particular who sat next to me that seemed to be nice, so I struck up a conversation with her. She told me her name was Rosemarie Kline. Rosemarie was very talkative and friendly. She had light blonde hair with soft blue eyes. She wore glasses and she reminded me of a smart, brainy kid you would want to know just in case you needed help with your school work. Although I considered myself a pretty smart kid, I didn't think it would hurt to have other smart friends. I think that's why Rosemarie and I got along so well on so many levels. We liked the same things: television programs, books, games and other activities that made us easily connect to each other.

We exchanged phone numbers and began calling one another after school every day. We would talk on the telephone for hours, laughing and recounting the day's events and anticipating the next day's activities. She and I had so many things in common it was hard to believe we had only met at the beginning of the school year. It is so funny how you can feel you have made a real connection with a person...but one unforeseen action can significantly change everything.

I can't remember anything out of the ordinary happening at school on this particular day that would have prompted a change. Rosemarie and I had lunch as usual, talked during some of our breaks, and made plans to talk later in the evening on the telephone. As usual, when I got home from school I did my homework, ate dinner, and got on the telephone with Rosemarie. We never talked about anything too serious, just a lot of girl talk and homework assignments. However, this time when I called her house something was different in her tone. I was told by Rosemarie that I could no longer call her house. This took me by surprise and I asked her, "Why? What is the problem?"

She hesitated and then said, "Taffnee, my parents said we could no longer be friends."

I think I was more stunned than anything because I did not understand the sudden change. During school that day, everything had gone well and there was no indication that a problem existed. I think that's why I took what felt like rejection so hard, because I couldn't understand where it was coming from, and how things could have changed so suddenly.

I persisted in asking Rosemarie, "What is the problem? Have I done something to hurt your feelings?" She insisted that there was no problem, but I could no longer call the house. I knew there was more she was not saying, but I thought she just didn't want to hurt my feelings.

The next thing I knew, her mom got on the phone and said words I will never forget, "We don't want any niggers calling our house!" Then the line went dead.

There I sat with my mouth wide open not knowing what to do or say. I couldn't believe what I had just heard. Somehow it didn't seem real to me. Tears began to stream down the sides of my face as the words reverberated in my head, "We don't want any niggers calling our house!" I hung up the phone and I went to my room.

I felt very ashamed and I didn't want anyone to know what had just happened. I knew what the word meant, but I never thought of myself in that way. I didn't understand how anyone could reject me – me of all people! – simply because of my skin color. I had seen things on TV, but I had never experienced anything like that in 12 years of existence. My parents never taught my sisters or me to dislike people or be prejudiced in any way, so this seemed to be a foreign concept to me. I figured I would have a chance to talk to Rosemarie at school on the next day and we would get everything cleared up, but that is not what happened.

When I got to school the next morning I did not see Rosemarie as usual. When I finally saw her, she was not as friendly as she had been in the past. I asked her why we couldn't be friends in school anyway regardless of what her parents had to say. I told her I did not have to call her house and she did not have to call my house, but we could remain friends at school. To my surprise, she told me that her parents did not want her to associate with me, or any Black person. Therefore, we could not be friends at any level.

I think I was more hurt because she was allowing her parents to pick her friends and just throw away the friendship I thought we had built over the past several months. I had been rejected because of my color – not because of anything I had done wrong. Color wasn't a thing I could change. Even if I could change it, I didn't want to anyway. I was perfectly happy with who I was, but this situation made me doubt myself. I felt lost, confused, hurt, rejected and all these other emotions I could not describe. This left me with an empty feeling so deep within my soul I didn't know how I would cope.

It's not like I didn't know any other White kids. The area where I grew up still had a small number of White families who remained in the community. I later learned most of the other White families had moved away during the period which is now referred to as,

"White Flight." At the time, I was too young to understand this fact; therefore, I thought everybody lived in the neighborhood because they liked it the same way I did. Although I didn't know it then, many of the other White families who used to live in the community had moved out as more Black people moved in, but I had no knowledge of this dynamic.

My parents had not taught me to pick my friends based on color, creed, religious preference, or any other bias that one could think of. On the contrary, my parents were always accepting of all kinds of people in our home. The White kids who lived in our neighborhood that visited our home were just as welcome as anyone else. Moreover, we had several children in the community who had physical and/or mental challenges, and we never saw a difference in how they were treated. That's why I think I never had a problem making friends with all types of people from all walks of life.

Making friends came easily for me, and I never had a problem being friendly to people who were friendly with me. Even if they weren't friendly first, I had no problem making the first move to be friendly. I guess that's why I took to Rosemarie – because she was friendly and pleasant to hang around. My color was never an issue as far as I knew.

She and I became fast friends when we met at the start of 7th grade. We would sit together at lunch, talk during study hall, hang out together at the after school-functions, and even talk about homework assignments on the telephone in the evenings. I thought the relationship was mutual between the two of us; no pretense, just two teen-aged girls talking about teen-age girl things. It never dawned on me that her parents would have a problem with me calling their home if they knew I was a Black girl.

I don't think the issue of my being Black ever came up in any of our conversations, and I am not sure what prompted the change. It seemed incomprehensible to me that Rosemarie's parents would not like me simply because of my color. My parents never taught me to dislike people based on color. My parents never had a problem with me being friends with people of a different race so I just assumed other parents felt the same way. Obviously, I was totally wrong about her parents. I don't know if Rosemarie knew how her parents felt and she chose to ignore them and be my friend anyway. Or, if she finally succumbed to their bias and made it her own. Regardless of the scenario, it caught me off guard and shattered my naiveté about people.

When I got home from school that afternoon, I think I went through the rest of the evening in a daze. I didn't know if I should talk with anyone about this situation, or if anyone else besides me had to face a scenario like this one.

Who would I talk to? How would I tell them that someone who I thought was my friend would no longer associate with me because I was a "Nigger?" I didn't dare talk to any of my neighborhood friends about it because I felt I might get ridiculed. Some people might even think I was trying to be "White" by hanging out with a White girl. All of my sisters were younger than me and I wasn't sure they would really understand either. As a 12-year-old with a limited perspective, the only thing I could think to do was maybe talk with my parents because it was beyond my comprehension and thought-level to tell anyone else. I didn't know if either of them could relate to what I was feeling. Who else could I turn to?

It took me a couple of days to digest what had happened to me, but I finally decided I needed to talk to someone who might be able to help me understand. When I got home from school that afternoon, my mom was at home, but my dad was still at work. I decided to talk to her first about this situation to see what advice she would give me. I just wanted to see what her response would be if I told her my friend Rosemarie had rejected me and no longer wanted to be friends because I was Black.

My mom was one of those no-nonsense kind of moms who did not believe in getting involved in "children's mess." She was a beautiful lady with a beautiful personality, but she was one of those matter-of-fact types of people who had a way of cutting to the chase. She was also one of those saved, sanctified, filled-with-the-Holy-Ghost people who believed in turning the other cheek and forgiving and letting the situation go.

Her attitude was: "Taffnee, it's not that serious." I understood what she was saying, but somehow it did not make me feel any better as she was talking. I knew she was correct, but it did not eliminate my feeling of unworthiness.

When my dad got home, I couldn't wait to tell him about the whole situation. I wanted to see what he would say. I think I am like the typical girl who thinks her dad is the smartest, bravest, most handsome man in all the world and I felt he would understand and relate to what I was saying more than my mom.

My dad was a very wise man, but not quite as "saved" as my mom. My dad worked as a police officer in our local city and I thought he would have a broader perspective about the situation. Not only was he knowledgeable, but he was very smart and a man of the world. So when I reiterated the story of what had happened to me, my dad said, "Taffnee, if she doesn't want to be your friend because you're Black, then you don't want to be her friend because she is White." Somehow his words resonated with me and made me feel better. I was beginning to think there was something wrong with me and I wasn't worthy of being her friend.

My dad continued to speak. "If her mom and dad feel that way about you and they don't even know you, they are ignorant. First of all, you have to realize White people are jealous of Black people and the only way they can express their jealousy is by trying to make you feel bad about yourself. She is no better than you and you don't want to be friends with anyone who doesn't want to be friends with you. There are a lot of ignorant people in the world and you can't live your life crying over what they say or think."

"Oh, my God!" I thought to myself. "He is right! I shouldn't be the one feeling bad because I've done nothing wrong."

His calm and matter-of-fact tone reassured me that I was going to be okay. He let me know I was just as important as anyone else and I had a family who loved me. He then said, "You are pretty, smart, friendly, got a great personality and anyone with sense would be proud to be your friend. Hold your head up high when you get back to school and ignore her. There's always someone else who wants to be your friend and will appreciate you for who you are."

Needless to say, I felt better hearing those words coming from my dad's mouth. Somehow I knew everything was going to be okay. Losing Rosemarie's friendship was a hard thing, but would be a life lesson that would help me become stronger. My friendship was worth more than some ignorant person boiling it down to my color. It reaffirmed in me that I was just as good as the next person and I had nothing to feel badly about. When I got to school the next day, equipped with my newly-found confidence, I felt ready for whatever came my way. I never spoke to Rosemarie again and I didn't feel bad about it. This situation taught me a very valuable lesson about prejudice and bigotry: It makes no sense.

The rest of the school year went by without a hitch. I soon forgot all about Rosemarie and my negative experience with her. I didn't allow my whole junior high school career to become over-shadowed by one mean comment. I proceeded to make other new friends who were just as nice as I thought Rosemarie was at the beginning. Before I knew it, I was leaving Southside and moving to Boca Ciega High School. Although this was a time of great racial turbulence, I managed to meet a lot of great people, both Black and White, at my high school. I worked very hard to keep an open mind regarding people of different races, but it was becoming increasingly more difficult to maintain my innocence about these matters when there was such a deep racial divide throughout the country.

As I look back now, I realize my parents were shielding me from many harsh realities that existed about race and prejudice. Once I got to high school, I began to witness firsthand the unpleasantness of bigotry that hid its ugly head underneath the surface of perceived tolerance. The years were fraught with racial tensions that ultimately left no one unscathed. Yet, through it all, I managed to keep a hopeful attitude that one day things would eventually get better.

Fast forward to 1987. By this time, I had been married for over 10 years to my handsome and charming husband, Marcell Johnson. Marcell and I had one beautiful son together who was smart, alert, outgoing, bouncy, and a joy to be around. Daniel was one of the most precious things I had in my life, and I had very high hopes and dreams for him—as all parents do.

I think that most of us parents are willing to do anything we can to ensure our children are exposed to a minimum number of negative situations and individuals. However, it is not always possible to shield our children from ignorance, no matter what their age. We hope that our children won't have to go through the same hurts and fears that we have had to face. It's been my experience that things don't change as much as they *appear* to change. Therefore, we must be ready when the unexpected happens.

Until the age of about two or three, my son went to a private babysitter while my husband and I went to work. When we changed him to a daycare setting, we checked out a few places that were recommended to us by friends who had children in our son's age group. The place we decided to send him was KinderCare, which was a small facility about two miles from our home, located in a very nice neighborhood. The daycare center was clean, modern and had a lot of great learning programs for children in preparation for kindergarten and grade school.

The director, Ms. Trudy Bolder, seemed to be a fine lady. Ms. Trudy was a middle-aged White woman with dark hair and blue eyes. She was a little plump around the middle, but she had a beautiful smile and a pleasant, easy manner that made you like her immediately.

Marcell and I visited the school and really liked the small classroom setting. Daniel was placed in a class with other three- and four-year-olds who were just as energetic as he was. The teacher was a young, White female by the name of Ms. Kathy Wells and she supervised approximately eight to ten other kids in the class. She appeared to be a nice young lady and the children seemed to like her very much. She looked like she was around 22 to 25 years of age and well able to handle the rambunctious group. She had a slender to medium build, dark hair, and dark eyes. She was attractive and seemed to have a pleasant enough personality.

I knew the first few days of being in a new school environment would require a little adjustment for Daniel. He had come from a home daycare situation which only had five other children who had known each other since they were infants. Daniel was now being placed in a larger classroom setting where he would be the only

Black child in the class. However, the other children seemed nice. I figured three and four-year-olds generally got along without too much prompting. The fact that he was the only Black child in the class didn't bother me too much because I knew Daniel made friends quickly and he was so pleasant to be around. How could anyone not like him?

I know the first week at a new school is always the toughest, but when Marcell and I came to pick up our son from daycare during that first week, I noted Daniel wasn't playing with the other children. I thought it might be because he was feeling a little lonesome for his other friends. I asked his teacher if there was any problem. Ms. Kathy said, "Daniel acts a little shy, but that is to be expected since he is the new kid in the class." Then she added: "He likes to play alone."

"You should make a little more effort to get him involved in the activities with the other children," I suggested.

"He participates just fine in the group activities," she replied. "But when it is time to go outside and play, he plays by himself or he sits in a corner."

Well, of course I thought Daniel just didn't know how to go about making friends, so I asked him, "Do you know any of the other kid's names in the class?"

"No."

"You've got to make an effort to get to know the other kids in the class by telling them your name and asking them their name."

"Okay."

Although I thought Ms. Kathy could have done a better job of ensuring our son's comfort in his new environment, I had no doubt our son would fit in with the other children and soon be running around with the best of them. I understood that Daniel was the new kid in the class and it might take a little time for him to adjust. I just thought his teacher could have made more of an effort to encourage involvement with the other students until he became more comfortable on his own.

I didn't think Ms. Kathy was as concerned about Daniel's social development as I was; otherwise, she would not have allowed him to play alone while the other children played group games. I felt I had talked with him enough so that he would make more of an effort to make friends, but it wasn't happening as fast as I thought it should. I knew that something was wrong, but I couldn't put my finger on the real problem. It didn't occur to me that it might be anything other than a normal adjustment period, but I would soon discover that there was something much more sinister than what I'd imagined.

After a couple of weeks, things seemed to be progressing along pretty well and Daniel wasn't sitting around by himself as much. A few days later when we picked Daniel up from school, he seemed to be adjusting well and had made a few friends. He was playing like the other kids. That made me very happy because I thought he was fitting in and learning how to socialize with others.

I couldn't think of anything that could go wrong. He was behaving like a three-year-old should behave and he was learning and participating with the best of them. However, one afternoon when Marcell and I came early to pick our son up from school, I found him sitting alone in the corner again. I asked him, "Why aren't you outside playing with the other kids?"

His reply took my breath away: "They don't want to play with me because I'm a nigger."

Marcell and I looked at each other in disbelief. I think we were both in shock. I couldn't believe my ears! Did he say what I thought he said? This couldn't be happening - not again, not with my son! It felt like déjà vu; a blast from the past that brought back a flood of bad memories to my mind. It was the situation with Rosemarie Kline all over again.

Could I have heard him incorrectly? I couldn't believe my three-year-old child had to face someone telling him they would not play with him because he was a "Nigger." This wasn't 1967, I thought to myself, but 1987. I was angry over what was said, but my biggest concern was that it had hurt my child.

Tears began streaming down my face before I knew it. Not only did I hurt for my son, but it took me back to my own childhood when those same words had been spoken to me. I could see the hurt in his eyes. I could understand the pain he felt. I don't even know if he really knew what those words meant, but I know he understood it meant something bad.

It also brought back the old hurt from my junior high school days when Rosemarie's mom had told me the same thing. Although I was much older than my son when I heard those words, I could remember the sting of rejection those ludicrous words delivered when Rosemarie's mom said them to me. They were meant to imply that being Black was something bad, even though I was older than my son had been and knew better. I didn't want my three-year-old to have to experience that hurt. The words are still harmful regardless of who says them; no matter the age of the person to whom they are directed.

Marcell immediately sprang into action and began to comfort Daniel. He let him know there was no need for him to feel bad because he was a very special boy. He also let him know we loved him and everything was going to be alright. He assured Daniel that none of this was his fault. Daniel seemed to feel better just by having us near. We encouraged him to go find a game to play while we spoke to his teacher Ms. Kathy.

When we found Ms. Kathy, she was outside with the other children. The first thing I wanted to know was what she would say when I asked her why Daniel was sitting inside the center by himself playing.

Ms. Kathy answered, "He said he didn't want to go outside and play." I then told her Daniel stated one of the children said they didn't want to play with him because he was a "Nigger." Her eyes bulged. She seemed genuinely surprised at this statement. "Mr. and Mrs. Johnson, I am so sorry. I never heard anyone say such a thing to Daniel. I hope you know I would never allow any child to say such a mean thing to another child. I can't imagine any of the children saying such a horrible thing like that to him."

"I hope you aren't implying that my son would make up such a thing."

"Absolutely not," she replied. "I just can't imagine where a little kid would get such a word from."

I could imagine where it might have come from. "I believe it had to come from an adult or the parents. I think these children are too young to think of such a thing on their own. Neither my husband nor I use such words around our son and we certainly don't want other children saying such things to him either."

Ms. Kathy then asked in a solemn voice if it would be okay to ask Daniel who said such a mean thing to him. Marcell and I agreed because we wanted to know also. Marcell went and got Daniel from the other classroom and brought him into the area where we were sitting. When we asked him who said the words to him, he replied, "John."

"I just can't believe John would say such a thing. I've never heard him use such language before." Ms. Kathy said. "I will speak to John and, again, I am very sorry."

I thanked her, but I told her I was going to talk with the Director, Ms. Trudy Bolder, to make sure that she knew what had happened in the class. Ms. Kathy said she understood our displeasure and apologized again.

When we left Ms. Kathy's classroom, the next stop was the office of Ms. Trudy Bolder. Although we had not had a lot of interaction with Ms. Trudy, we would see her in the mornings and evenings when we came in to pick up Daniel. Usually she was somewhere around assuring things went smoothly, and she seemed to be a kind person.

I did not know how she would react upon hearing what we had to say, but Ms. Trudy had to be told. I wanted to make sure she spoke to John's parents as well as Ms. Kathy to find out what was really going on. I knew John did not come to such a conclusion on his own. He was too young to think in those terms, and I was pretty sure something like this had to come from home. Regardless of where he got it, it had to be addressed.

When I spoke to Ms. Trudy, she was shocked to hear something like that happened in one of her classrooms and she was very apologetic. She said she would speak to the little boy's parents to let them know what happened. She wanted to make sure they understood such behavior was unacceptable and would not be tolerated at the school. She also said that she would talk with Ms. Kathy to find out why she was unaware of what was going on in her classroom.

Ms. Trudy also seemed to be very concerned about Daniel. She did not want this one incident to have a negative impact on him or color his view of the world. She did not want us to have a negative feeling about the school. Ms. Trudy said, "I assure you, Mr. and Mrs. Johnson, that this situation will be handled immediately when John's mom comes by to pick him up. I don't want anyone to think I run the kind of school where prejudice is tolerated. I want to make sure nothing like this ever happens to another student again."

I truly felt Ms. Trudy was sincere and she understood our feelings. I could see she felt genuinely hurt over the whole situation and I knew it would be taken care of without hesitation. I had no hard feelings against the little boy because I knew he was only repeating what he had heard. However, I knew something had to be done so he would never repeat something like that again.

I knew when we got home that I would have to have "The Talk" with Daniel about prejudice and discrimination. I never thought I would have to have this talk with my son at this early stage of life. I really hoped that we as a Country had evolved a little bit more and had moved past some of this ignorance since 1967, but I knew in my heart of hearts we had not.

The light bulb came on in my head and I knew what I had to do. My mind went back to the words my dad spoke to me and I knew immediately what I had to say to Daniel. I wanted to do for my son the same thing my dad had done for me over 20 years ago - make him understand there was nothing wrong with him. I felt fully enlightened and ready to tackle the situation head-on. God had already prepared me with the words I needed to say.

I understood it was going to be a little more challenging to explain the concept of prejudice to Daniel because he was only three. However, I needed to make the analogies relevant and comprehendible for someone so young. Marcell and I thought about trying to ignore the situation and act as though it never happened, but we both knew that was not the right way to deal with it. Our first priority was to make sure Daniel was okay, both mentally and physically. The truth is that in a couple of years, he might not even remember the entire incident, but we were concerned about his self-esteem and body-image at the current time. Consequently, we knew something had to be said.

I started the conversation by telling him, "God made people in all colors for a reason. God also made flowers in many different colors as well. There was no bad color and they were all beautiful. You are a beautiful little brown boy and anyone would be proud to be your friend. There are a lot of jealous people in the world, but don't let jealous people make you sad. Sometimes people want what you have and when they can't get it, they try to make you feel bad."

He asked, "Do you think John wants to be brown like me?"

"Yes, that's why he said what he said. He knows you are even smarter than he is and he knows the other children will like you just as much when they get to know you. Tomorrow when you get to school, be nice. If no one wants to play with you, just find something you like to do and have fun doing it. Someone else will want to have fun with you. I guarantee you that."

Daniel seemed to take it all in stride, as much as a three-year-old can do. I gave him a great big hug and kiss, and reminded him that his dad and I loved him very much. "You are our special little boy and we love you no matter what." That seemed to be enough for him. Just knowing that his dad and I were there to love him and protect him from the bad things in life made him feel better.

The other amazing thing was that I remembered the words my dad had spoken to me, and I was now repeating them to my son. I was able to provide him with the same comfort I felt when my dad talked to me so many years ago.

The next day when we brought Daniel for school, Ms. Trudy called me aside. "Mrs. Johnson, I had the opportunity to speak with John's mom about the incident with Daniel. She said she did not know where John would have gotten such a thing from, but she would talk with him anyway. She said she would let him know what he said was wrong and he should never say anything like that again." Ms. Trudy looked me in the eye, then continued, "I let her know we treat all our children the same regardless of race, creed, or color. We want every child to have a great experience at the school."

I thought for a minute, then said, "Didn't sound like the mom denied her son said what Daniel said he said."

"She didn't deny it, but she acted like she was surprised he said it at school."

"I'm not surprised," I replied, "especially if that is the way the parents feel. The boy is bound to repeat what he has heard at home."

Ms. Trudy nodded in agreement. "I assure you that I will not ignore this incident and I have spoken with all my staff to make sure they know nothing like this will be tolerated from the parents, children, or the staff."

I thanked her for her discrete and prompt handling of the situation. I felt good about leaving my son in her care.

John's parents eventually withdrew him from the school and probably sent him to a private school. That was certainly their right, just as it was my right to protect my son from negative influences. Additionally, I think Ms. Kathy left the school because I don't remember seeing her too much longer after that incident. Daniel remained at KinderCare until he started first grade. As far as I know he never had any other problems at the school with prejudice or mistreatment. I am glad we were able to intervene before any ill will could develop and change the man Daniel would ultimately become.

Daniel is now a man with a son and daughter of his own, and I don't even think he remembers the incident. I hope he never has to have the prejudice talk with his children like I had to have with him. However, if he does, I know he is ready to reassure them of their value and worth even though others would have them think differently. Having someone there to shield you from the ills of life today helps to ensure a healthy and strong tomorrow. Someone once said, "It's not what people call you that matters; but it's what you answer to that makes the difference."

As I look back in retrospect, I never really knew what happened to Rosemarie after that last conversation, but I do know I did not see her in my classes anymore. Her parents may have withdrawn her from the school. They may have sent her to a private school or to another school that did not have any Black children in it. I don't presume to know how her life progressed or what she has become as an adult, but I hope she has had time to reflect and make what happened a positive learning experience just like I did. This situation could have easily left me with a jaded view of White people, but God used it to help me prepare for my future.

Although this might be considered a negative experience by some people, I think this encounter helped me prepare myself for future episodes I might confront later in life. I have learned that everyone has negative life experiences, but it's what you do about them that matters.

The real lesson I learned was forgiveness. I forgave Rosemarie and her parents for their ignorance, but I also forgave John because he was too young to understand the impact of his words. I don't know if I thought of my feelings in terms of forgiveness after my friendship ended with Rosemarie, but I knew I could not allow those words to control the rest of my life and color my future relationships with other people. Having forgiveness enabled me to learn the lesson without leaving me bitter and broken.

I am so glad I have had the opportunity to become more enlightened about life, people, and the real meaning of friendship. I have learned that a true friend cares for you regardless of what others may say or think. It doesn't matter what your color, background, education level, economic level, or any of the other unimportant things people may use to judge you.

The most important thing is to know who you are and W*hose* you are. God made me a beautiful, smart, and strong Black woman and I have no need to apologize for that. I can be happy without any doubt about who I am. I do not feel ashamed because of what God made me to be…a proud Black woman.

PART II

The Crazy Sex Story

In the summer of 1973, I was a proud and bubbly high school graduate. My plans were to eventually enroll in college at some point, but I decided to attend St. Petersburg Vocational & Technical Institute (Vo-Tech) in the upcoming fall semester. Having recently graduated, I wasn't sure what I wanted to do with the rest of my life. I knew I wanted to go to college at some point, but I wasn't sure what I wanted my major to be.

I had a passion for writing, music, and singing. I'd had aspirations of being an opera singer or a ballet dancer, but those dreams were dashed many years before. Therefore, I thought learning a trade might be my best avenue to obtaining a skill and finding a real job. I wanted to learn a trade that would make me more marketable, pay me more money, and lead to a long term career.

I was very fortunate because my parents never put pressure on me to get a job, nor were they rushing me out of the house. Consequently, I had time to figure out what I really wanted to do with my life. I was one of the fortunate girls who did not have any children, so I only had to be responsible for myself. I wasn't married and had no intentions of getting married anytime soon, so I could focus on my own goals. I had given my life to the Lord. My life consisted of going to school, work and church. I dated here and there, but mainly, I was figuring out what I wanted to do with myself for the future. I knew I would eventually want to move out of my parent's home and get my own place; therefore, I had to start making preparations to meet my goals as soon as possible.

Even though I was planning to attend the Vo-Tech in the fall, I had no idea what trade I was interested in learning. I consulted a counselor at the Vo-Tech so I could get some advice about potential fields of study. I decided on Data Processing and Keypunch Operation. I was told that this was an up-and-coming field in which I could more readily get a job.

Moreover, working in an office sounded like something suitable for me to do as a long-term career. I had my plan of action already outlined and all I had to do was wait on the fall semester to begin so I could start taking classes.

I have always been an enterprising person. I'd started working as a weekend babysitter for a few family members and friends around the neighborhood while in high school. I liked making money and having the ability to buy extra things my parents couldn't afford to buy me. My sisters and I received a little allowance, but babysitting gave me a little extra change in my purse. It was an okay job, but I wanted to earn a little more money than I could make working as a babysitter on the weekends. So I found a part-time job at Aunt Hattie's Restaurant to earn some extra cash.

This was the first time I had worked for a real company rather than a friend or family member. I was hired as a bus-girl. Although I had never worked in a restaurant before, I figured it wouldn't be too hard. My job entailed removing dirty dishes from the table and cleaning the table and setting it up for the next customer. The job wasn't a very difficult job, but it was pretty demanding at times. I knew how to remove dishes and clean a table, but working at a fast pace was a little more challenging for me.

I didn't have a problem clearing the table of dirty dishes and wiping it down, but transporting the pan full of dirty dishes back to the kitchen was always a problem. Sometimes the pans got dropped and dishes got broken. Then I would have to help clean up the broken glass from the mess I made. I didn't break things all the time, but I broke enough things that my manager was not too pleased with my performance.

Needless to say, I didn't like the work as much as I thought I would. I enjoyed working with people, but I could tell my boss didn't think I was very good at my job. While it satisfied my need to earn money, I was relieved when I eventually lost the position because I knew that I didn't want restaurant work to be my life's vocation.

I moved on to a part-time job at the Southside Nursing Facility. It was a great way to make some money and give me something positive to do before school started. I knew the job at the nursing home would not be a lifelong career either, but I could earn some extra cash to help me with school expenses. I thought my job working at the nursing home would be a lot easier than working in a restaurant because I wouldn't be moving at such a fast pace. This was going to be a job that would help me earn a little extra money and maybe even learn how to work in a real business environment without undue pressure.

When I started working at the nursing home I found the job to be very similar to my first job at Aunt Hattie's Restaurant. It wasn't a very difficult job and it wasn't quite as demanding as restaurant work. I worked in the kitchen washing dishes and setting up trays of food to serve the seniors who ate in the dining room. I also had to clean the tables once the seniors were done eating. The main skills I needed for this job was speed and accuracy; however, I didn't seem to possess either of these skills with any proficiency. It seemed to me that I was always breaking something and dropping something, just like at my last job. Consequently, I knew my tenure at this job probably wasn't going to be that long, but I gave it the good old college try. I worked as hard as I could to do a good job and make it work despite my shortcomings.

The one positive thing I had going for me is that no matter where I went or what I did, I always had the potential for making friends. I made friends easily because I never seemed to meet a stranger. I never allowed age, race, religion or any other factors about a person sway my attitude. My philosophy was, "If you are nice to me, I will be nice to you," and that always seemed to work. I always tried to be patient and respectful to the seniors I was serving and honor their requests as much as possible. I liked people and generally people liked me.

While working in the kitchen, I met a young woman by the name of Catalina Jones. She was the kitchen manager who was responsible for food preparation and maintenance of the kitchen facilities. Part of her responsibilities included training me so that I could assist her with the task of serving the seniors who were able to come to the dining room and eat their meals. I also washed dishes, swept and mopped the kitchen floor, and helped set up things for the next day. We worked well together and this made the job more tolerable and fun for me. I liked working with her because she was easy to get along with. She and I became pretty close because we worked together on a daily basis.

As I continued to work with Catalina over the next few months, I found out through conversation she had been married, but was now divorced. She also had a little girl by the name of Olivia who was her pride and joy. Although I was just a part-time worker, she took me under her wing like she was my big sister. She wanted to help me learn and succeed. I am sure she realized I wasn't going to be working at the facility for too long, and that's why she probably gave me the opportunity to baby-sit for her sometimes on the weekends. I know I wasn't the most efficient worker when it came to kitchen duty, but I was an outstanding babysitter who loved children.

At this time in my life, I probably wouldn't be considered very worldly because I led a pretty sheltered life by most standards. I think my mom and dad did an outstanding job raising my five siblings and me without any major problems. I had proven myself to be a pretty mature girl, so they trusted my judgment about most things. I think Catalina knew I was a responsible and trustworthy person that's why she allowed me to care for her most prized possession, Olivia. I exhibited good home-training and I appeared to have my head on straight. I think that's why Catalina wanted to help me.

The only reason I started working jobs outside of baby-sitting was to earn money to buy the extra things I wanted for school. Also, I liked expensive clothes, shoes, and personal items that my parents weren't willing to purchase. Therefore, it was incumbent upon me to work if I wanted these things. By all accounts I was considered a typical teenaged girl with all the fluff and stuff that goes along with the gender.

I would probably also not be considered one of the bravest people in the world, but I am not the most fearful, either. I have never been afraid to try new things, even if they didn't work out to my advantage. I considered every opportunity a new chance to learn something I didn't already know.

I had worked as a babysitter for a few close family members and friends around the neighborhood so this babysitting job with Catalina was nothing new.

Catalina and her daughter lived on one side of a two-bedroom duplex right off of 22nd Avenue South. It was a little bit further away than most of my other babysitting jobs, but I was close enough to access help if I needed it. Her apartment consisted of a living room/dining room combination, a small kitchen, one bathroom and two bedrooms. I assumed the other side was laid out the same since I had never been in it before.

Additionally, I noted that the neighborhood seemed to be pretty quiet and I felt comfortable staying there alone with Olivia. I have always thought of myself as a rational thinking person and I don't usually jump to outlandish conclusions without some provocation. It gave me comfort to know my family wasn't too far away if I needed help. All I had to do was to call if I needed them.

Olivia was about five years old, and very cute. She was soft spoken, curious, and funny. I really loved babysitting for Olivia because she was well-trained and easy to handle. The first time I babysat for Catalina's daughter, everything went off without a hitch. It was easy to keep her happy because she enjoyed playing games and listening to bedtime stories. I had no trouble getting her to bed on time. Once she was safely tucked in bed and off to sleep, I could relax, watch TV, or talk on the telephone and wait for Catalina to return home. This was an easy and fun way to make a little extra money.

One evening Catalina called and asked if I could babysit Olivia for her. Everything started out great, as usual. Olivia and I played some games and then I read her a bedtime story. After Olivia fell asleep, I decided I would watch a little TV. There seemed to be nothing too interesting on TV to watch so I got up and went into the kitchen and found myself a Coke and some potato chips to munch on while I waited for Catalina to return. After enjoying my snack, I think I must have dozed off to sleep. I don't think I had been asleep for very long before I was awakened by a strange sound.

"Scrunch, scrunch, scrunch…" In my subconscious mind I could hear the noise, but I couldn't figure out what the sound was or where it was coming from. I became a little nervous. It sounded like something was scratching on the wall or chewing on something. I couldn't tell, and I was too afraid to open my eyes right away.

I heard the noise again. Startled and fully awakened, I listened more intently to figure out where the sound was coming from. It wasn't a constant noise, but the rate would change. Sometimes going faster; sometimes going slower. "Scrunch scrunch scrunch…scrunch…scrunch scrunch scrunch scrunch…" It almost had a rhythmic quality, but unlike anything I had ever heard. I thought to myself, "What in the world is going on?"

I opened my eyes and looked around to make sure no one had gotten into the apartment while I was asleep. As I slowly panned my surroundings, it appeared that no one was in the apartment but me and Olivia. I jumped up from the sofa quickly and I checked to make sure she was okay. She appeared to be sleeping peacefully, but I still could not figure out what the strange scrunching noise was, or where it was coming from. All of a sudden the noise stopped and there was silence again. However, it had un-nerved me as I continued to look around the room.

I thought perhaps it might be a rat or mouse inside the wall. It seemed to be coming from behind the TV. I cautiously moved towards the TV to see if there was anything there. I didn't want to be caught off-guard by some small rodent jumping out to chase me. I am not quite sure what I expected, but I didn't have an exit plan prepared, and I wasn't sure how I was going to protect Olivia if my fears were justified.

As I moved slowly towards the television, panning my eyes from side to side, I didn't see anything unusual. After checking thoroughly behind the TV, I found nothing there either. I didn't know what else to do or think. The sound defied any logical explanation I could imagine. It seemed a little funny to me that this scrunching sound would start and stop; go faster and sometimes go slower, but I couldn't think what the noise could be. The more I listened; I soon thought it must be something going on in between the walls of the two apartments.

There were only low sounds of talking on the other side of the wall, and I certainly did not hear anything they were saying or doing that I thought could be making these sounds.

I didn't know the neighbors, so I didn't feel comfortable bothering them if the noise turned out to be nothing but noisy pipes. I didn't have a number to call Catalina, but I knew where she was spending the evening. I didn't want to disrupt her evening with an over-active imagination and being overly dramatic. Since I didn't know what was happening, I thought to be on the safe side, I'd better call my dad so he could have a look around.

The best thing about where Catalina lived was that it was about 5 minutes driving time from where my parents lived. I knew it would not take my dad long to get to us once I made the call. I felt better just knowing my dad was going to stop by the apartment. My dad was a big strapping, strong guy who was knowledgeable and smart. He was also a long-time police officer, and I was very confident he would know what to do if something shady was going on.

While I waited for my dad to arrive, I decided to turn on all the lights in the apartment, with the exception of the light in Olivia's room. I certainly didn't want to awaken her or unnecessarily alarm her either. Fortunately for me it didn't take my dad long to get to the apartment to check around. However, it was awfully funny that by the time he got there the sounds had stopped and everything had gotten quiet again. When my dad came into the apartment, he took a look around. He didn't find anything out of place or any apparent signs of trouble. He reassured me everything was okay and I had nothing to worry about. Although my fears were unfounded, I was still glad my dad had stopped by to check everything out for me. Everything looked good to him so I could finally relax until Catalina returned.

I felt better after my dad left, but it was still a mystery to me as to what could be causing those scrunching noises, but I figured I would put it out of my mind for the time being. I didn't even mention the noises to Catalina when she returned home because it turned out to be nothing important. There appeared to be no danger so it wasn't worth mentioning. I don't remember ever hearing that sound again and I couldn't even sufficiently explain what I heard even if I tried.

I thought the best thing I could do would be to put this incident out of my mind whenever I came to Catalina's apartment to babysit Olivia. I just assumed she never heard the noise. Every now and then, I would remember this strange sound, but I couldn't come up with any rational reason for the sounds. I figured some things were just meant to be mysteries and this noise was one of them.

After that strange night at Catalina's house, I seldom thought about that noise again. It was just an event that happened, but had no real significance to me. It wasn't something that made me nervous or scared when I thought about it, but it did puzzle me. I never had any negative thoughts or apprehensions about returning to Catalina's house. I had virtually put it out of my head and would only think about it in passing. I concluded it was just one of those unexplained things that happen in life that doesn't really mean anything important. Moreover, it doesn't cause you to have a bad dream or memory, yet it can leave you puzzled because you can't explain it.

By the end of the summer I had earned a nice sum of money to help with books, supplies, and other things I wanted to buy. I attended the Vo-Tech and completed my certificate in Data Processing and Keypunch Operation. I never actually found employment in this field, but I found employment at one of the local banks. It was a pretty decent job and I didn't have to clean tables or wash dishes. I thought I might have an opportunity to advance, but by this time, I knew I was going to need a college degree if I was going to become a real professional.

It was at this time I decided to attend St. Petersburg Junior College. I decided to major in Police Administration with the possibility of one day becoming a lawyer. I had been attending the college for about a year when I met a nice guy by the name of Marcell Johnson. I thought I had my life all figured out, and it didn't include a long-term relationship. I wanted to be a career woman; doing my own thing and making my own decisions. I really didn't think I was ready to get married anytime soon, but Marcell and I hit it off fairly quickly and one year later we were getting married. Sometimes your plan for your life is not the same plan God has for your life, so you have to remain open to the possibility He knows best.

At the time we met, Marcell wasn't a student at the junior college, but he soon enrolled and started taking classes towards earning his accounting degree. Once I completed my A. A. Degree in Police Administration, I moved over to the University of South Florida and completed my B. A. Degree in Criminology. Marcell and I were well on our way to making a great life together. Everything in my life was moving forward and the event from that night when I babysat for Olivia had long since faded from the forefront of my mind. I was on my way to a great life and career with Marcell and everything was looking up.

After graduating from the University of South Florida, Marcell and I moved to Tallahassee where we both attended Florida State University. Once I completed my Master's Degree in Public administration, I accepted a job in Pensacola, Florida with the Naval Air Rework Facility (NARF). Since I had a job offer, Marcell decided he would complete his Accounting Degree at the University of West Florida. After graduation, we packed up and move to Pensacola. Although I accepted this job in Pensacola, I never expected to live there for more than a couple of years. I thought once Marcell finished his degree he would find a job in a different city. However, it turned out to be a place we would spend over 28 years building a great life and family.

When we moved to Pensacola, we lived in an apartment for a couple of years before finding our first home. We already had a lot of the furniture we needed to fill the space. The bedroom suite we had was given to us by my mom and dad when we first got married. Most of the things we had were in very good shape. The bedroom set was nice consisting of a full-sized bed, dresser with mirror, chest of drawers and a night stand. We had been sleeping on the same bed since we got married over 8 years ago and I decided it was time to get a new mattress, box spring and headboard. We didn't necessarily want to change the dresser or chest, but we wanted a larger bed. Marcell and I just wanted to move up to a queen-sized or king-sized bed because we thought it would be more roomy and comfortable.

Not long after settling in our new home our first son Daniel was born. He was a beautiful bouncing baby boy and he was the light of our lives. Daniel was probably about a year old when we started looking to upgrade our bed from a full-sized bed to a king- or queen- sized bed. Like most new parents, we allowed our son to sleep in the bed with us periodically, even though he had his own bed and room. Daniel was starting to get bigger, and a full-sized bed was not going to be as comfortable if he wanted to lie in the bed with us from time to time, so we needed to do something.

The hunt was on to find just the right bed. The master bedroom was a pretty large room that could accommodate a king- or queen-sized bed without a problem. It didn't take us long to find a nice headboard that would work well for either a king or queen frame. We then found a nice queen mattress and box spring set that seemed to fit the headboard very well.

We were very proud of our purchase and couldn't wait for it to be delivered to the house in a few days.

The mattress and box spring were delivered to us on the following Saturday afternoon, and it looked very good in the spot we had picked for it. After completing our daily tasks, we proceeded to get ready for bed. Daniel was already sleeping in his own room and I was excited about trying the new bed. I wasn't just excited because it was a new bed, but I was excited because it was a little larger than our old bed. Additionally, it gave us more room to move around and enjoy.

That night after we turned off the light, Marcell asked me, "How does the mattress feel to you?"

"Great!", I said, and then I asked him what he thought about it.

"I like it as well."

We started to cuddle with one another and it moved to a wonderful encounter of love- making. There was very little talking going on because we were in the groove where passion takes over and nothing needs to be said. All of a sudden we got into a sexual rhythm and the bed made a very distinct sound, "Scrunch scrunch scrunch. scrunch…scrunch…scrunch scrunch scrunch scrunch…"

As we continued to move in a rhythmic pattern on the bed, the scrunching noise of the mattress and headboard created something like a musical sound for the activity that was occurring. It was a cacophony of sound that definitely had a distinct cadence and beat. The light bulb in my head came on and all of a sudden I knew what the scrunching noises represented so many years ago!

I felt enlightened. It became crystal clear. I knew exactly what it was and there was no doubt in my mind what had been happening so long ago. My thoughts took me back to 1973 when I was baby-sitting for Olivia and I heard this same noise.

Now I understood! It all made sense! The people next door to Catalina were having sex. As Marcell and I came to a blissful climax, I could do nothing but laugh to myself at how naive and silly I was to the things of the world. I thought to myself, "How could you be so dumb? How could you not know what was happening?" But the only thing I could think in my defense was that I just didn't know. It brought to my mind how green I really was at that time. I laughed to myself, "I'm so glad our son is just a baby."

I realized after a few minutes of thinking back I had to get back into the present. However, as we lay there holding each other, my body started shaking uncontrollably with laughter. I was laughing so hard to myself as the full memory of that night came flooding back to my mind. As I continued laughing, Marcell wanted to know, "What is so funny?" I started trying to tell him the story, but I was so tickled and embarrassed to know how innocent I was back then. I could hardly get the story out of my mouth without laughing hysterically at my own naiveté.

Once I finished telling him the story, he had to laugh too. Marcell said, "Taffnee, you really didn't know what was happening in the apartment next door to where you were babysitting?"

"I know it's hard to believe that I couldn't figure out what was going on and what that sound could possibly have been; but I couldn't."

Marcell asked, "You haven't ever heard your mom and dad having sex before? You never walked in on them or even guessed what was happening?"

"I've never heard them to my knowledge or recollection. I am sure I knew they did it, Marcell, but somehow I never gave it much thought; and I certainly never heard scrunching noises coming from their room."

"Well, Taffnee, this is just a natural thing that goes on between a man and a woman and sometimes a bed can make noise."

"Marcell, how come our bed has never made that kind of noise before?"

"Maybe because it wasn't time for you to know what was happening until now." I thought maybe he was right. Until that point, I wasn't ready to know or understand what the people next door to Catalina were really doing.

Even though I was glad I finally knew what that crazy noise was from my young adult years, I guess you know my mind was made up that this wasn't the right bed for us. I figured if it made so much noise that people could figure out what was going on in the bedroom, unless they were dumb like me, then I felt sure my son would figure it out too. I certainly didn't want that happening. Not that I was so afraid of him knowing that his dad and I loved each other and we expressed that love by having sex, but I figured this was personal and we could explain the facts of life to him when the time was right. He needed to have his own sexual experiences to remember, not ours.

In retrospect, it's amazing to me that it took all those years for the light to finally come on in my mind about what was going on in the apartment next door to Catalina. It's hard to believe something as simple as making love on a squeaky bed could have me so puzzled and perplexed for so many years. It just didn't seem feasible. The questions I kept asking myself were: "What am I supposed to learn from this experience? Could God be using a simple situation like this to show me some important mystery? What is the ultimate point for this memory surfacing at that particular time in my life?"

I have often thought of this incident and wondered what could be so significant that it would remain in my subconscious mind all this time. I can't remember having any bad dreams or anxiety over what I heard. Yet, from time to time, I would remember the sound in my head as though it was yesterday. It remained a mystery to me until that night when I finally became enlightened. I guess there are things we aren't meant to know or understand until we are ready to accept the complexity of what we know.

I think the final take-away from my experience is appreciation. I have a profound appreciation for my family, my upbringing, my education, and my friends. The mind has an interesting way of compartmentalizing memories and events that happen to us. Things we have long since forgotten can suddenly be brought back to the forefront of our mind at the right time. Even if we don't fully realize it, activities and events have a connection in our lives; our minds will help us to draw connections that might not occur to us naturally.

I think God used this simple event to teach me a deeper spiritual lesson I can readily share with others. The one thing I do know for sure is that God does have a sense of humor. I know information about scx was readily available to me, but I probably wasn't ready to know it at the time.

Another thing I have learned is how to appreciate the importance of timing. Timing is everything. Knowing the right things at the right time is the best way to create sustained success. If you obtain knowledge too soon before you are ready and able to use it, that knowledge can be just as dangerous as not having the right knowledge when you need it.

Obviously, there were things I didn't need to know about sex during my babysitting years, but when the time was right, God revealed it to me.

Now Marcell and I have solved our squeaky bed problem - because you never know who might be listening. Enlightenment is all about learning what you need to know when you need to know it, regardless how insignificant it may seem.

ENLIGHTENMENT

PART III

The Big Fight

In 1978, I was a student at the University of South Florida, where I planned to obtain my Bachelor's Degree in Criminology. I had completed my A. A. degree in Police Administration and transferred over to the University of South Florida for further study. I had been taking classes at the University for about a year and I considered myself a pretty seasoned student. I obtained a work-study position in the office of Dr. Bruce Levi, who was a Political Science instructor. During those days most of the professors shared offices. Dr. Levi shared his office with another professor by the name of Dr. Angus Zachery. I enjoyed working for Dr. Levi because he was always pleasant and had an easy going manner. Dr. Zachery was a little more aloof, but he seemed to be okay as well.

I worked for Dr. Levi about 20 hours per week. My job was one in which I could perform my duties around my class schedule. I only had about two or three more quarters to go before I would finish my Bachelor's Degree. Although I had been working for Dr. Levi for only a few quarters, I enjoyed the work very much. My title was "Student Assistant," and my duties included filing, making copies, and answering the telephone. There was nothing difficult about the job, and Dr. Levi was very easy to get along with. He had a quick smile and a friendly demeanor. He was also tall and rather handsome, in a "professorly" sort of way.

As I stated earlier, Dr. Levi shared an office with Dr. Angus Zachery. Dr. Zachery appeared to be more of the young hippie-type professor. He had a medium build, dark hair and brown eyes. He was not particularly friendly, but not necessarily unfriendly either. He went about his daily routine with confidence and commitment. He never went out of his way to say anything to me, other than to offer a cordial greeting, and I did the same. I had no real interaction with him other than working in the office he shared with my supervisor. Therefore, our contact was very limited.

This was a pretty small campus, but I knew a lot of people, including students, professors, and workers. I had established myself as a good student, a hard worker, and a socially adept individual. That's why I think I got the opportunity to meet and befriend Dr. Timothy Carlson.

Dr. Carlson was the only Black professor working on our campus at the time. Since he was a new arrival in our city, I had the privilege of introducing him around the campus to other members of the student body and familiarizing him with the broader St. Petersburg Community. He taught in the Accounting Department and I had a chance to learn a lot from our association.

I knew very few Black Ph.Ds, and to have the opportunity to show Dr. Carlson around, I thought, was quite impressive. This gave me the feeling I could one day become somebody important too. Because I was picked to show Dr. Carlson around, versus some other student, it meant I had made a good impression on somebody. I thought my association with Dr. Carlson gave me clout, as well as a certain kind of respect with the student body. I was not only working for who I thought was a prominent professor, but I could see myself potentially moving in those circles as a professor myself one day. I could see nothing but good things happening in my future and I was excited to be me.

I had established a pretty standard routine of attending classes in the mornings and working for Dr. Levi in the afternoons. When I arrived at work on this particular afternoon, Dr. Levi was not in the office. Since I already knew what my assignment was for that day, I walked in the office, sat down at my desk, put my things in the desk drawer, and began to work as usual.

I wasn't sure where Dr. Levi was at that time, but Dr. Zachery soon came into the office.

I spoke to him as usual and he spoke back in a cordial manner. A few minutes later, a student came in to see him and they began to talk.

I heard the young student say to Dr. Zachery in a stern voice, "I don't want to take this class. I had a really hard schedule this past quarter and I am looking for an easy class to lighten my load for the next quarter."

Dr. Zachery told the young man, "You need this class and this is the best time for you to take it. You need to get it out of the way before you go any further." However, the young man persisted in his argument that he did not want to take the class that Dr. Zachery was recommending.

The level of their voices had elevated to a point that I could hear their entire conversation. I said, "Excuse me" and they stopped talking. They both turned and looked in my direction. "I have a suggestion for a class that I think would be easier and more enjoyable for you." With a big smile on my face I continued, "I think it would probably be the kind of class you are looking for to give you a lighter load for the next quarter."

The young man was interested. "What class are you talking about?"

"The class is a literature class that requires reading novels that are very interesting and fun." I felt like I was being helpful and thought this class would work well for the young man.

Dr. Zachery turned to the young man, "I don't think this is a good idea. You really need to take the class I have recommended."

The young man was excited about the literature class, though, and he said he wanted to find out more about it. As they continued to discuss his schedule, I got up from my desk and went out of the office to take a break.

When I returned to my desk approximately fifteen minutes later the young man was gone and Dr. Zachery had an angry look on his face that had not been there before I left. He told me, "I want you out of this office immediately."

I am sure I had a puzzled look on my face, because I couldn't understand the sudden change in his attitude. As I walked around him to go to my desk, he raised his voice, "Get your things and get out of this office right now!"

"Excuse me, Dr. Zachery? What are you talking about? I have work to do."

He then started flinging his arms wildly and said, "I mean I want you out of this office right now or I'll pick you up and throw you out!" His anger continued to rise, "I want you out of this office immediately!"

I couldn't figure out why he would be so angry with me after only a short time away from my desk. I asked him, "What is your problem? What have I done to you?"

He was furious, and he repeated his threat, "I don't want you in this office and if you don't leave right now, I will pick you up and throw you out!"

Needless to say, I was stunned and in total dismay at his venomous attitude. I couldn't believe what I was hearing and I couldn't think of anything I had done that would precipitate his actions. I was confused by the change in his demeanor and his tone. He was never that friendly, but he had always been cordial and civil. At this point, he was red-faced and hysterical.

I didn't know if he would actually try and pick me up and throw me out of the office, but his demeanor indicated he was serious.

In a loud, stern voice I said to him, "I don't work for you and I don't know what's wrong with you! Are you crazy?"

He was screaming at this point, "Get out of this office! Get out now or I will drag you out!"

I was so nervous and upset, I could hardly hold back the tears. I didn't want him to know how intimidated I felt, but I did not want to get into a physical altercation with him either. I wasn't sure if he would really do what he said he was going to do, and I didn't want to take any chances. I wasn't in the habit of fighting, and I certainly wasn't used to fighting a man.

I know we were both speaking in loud tones because Dr. Zachery had been yelling at the top of his lungs, but then, he made a move toward me. I thought he was going to physically handle me. I could see by this time there were other teachers and students who had come out into the hall to see what was going on. I quickly grabbed my purse from the desk and ran out of the office in tears.

As I rushed down the hallway, people were asking me what had happened. I couldn't even get the words out of my mouth without a flood of tears pouring from my eyes. I couldn't even explain because I didn't understand myself what was going on. The only thing I could think to do was go down to Dr. Carlson's office to get help from him. When I arrived, he wasn't there. As I was leaving Dr. Carlson's office, I saw him coming down the hallway and he immediately asked me what was wrong. I was crying so hysterically at this time that I could hardly explain what happened. I told him there was a fight between me and Dr. Zachery and he threatened to physically remove me from the office if I did not leave on my own. He then asked me what happened.

I told him I didn't know what happened. It made no sense to me and I couldn't explain it. All I could figure out was Dr. Zachery had gone berserk and I didn't understand why.

Dr. Carlson then asked me to take a seat and try to calm myself while he attempted to find Dr. Zachery. He told me to stay in his office so I could collect myself and he would attempt to get to the bottom of the situation. He wasn't gone very long, and once he returned to his office, he said he wasn't able to get Dr. Zachery to explain his actions because he appeared to be too upset to make sense out of the whole situation. There were still a lot of teachers and students milling around outside of Dr. Zachery's office, but none of them were sure what precipitated this altercation.

In the meantime, someone found Dr. Levi and told him what was going on at his office. He found me still sitting in Dr. Carlson's office. As he entered the room, he had a concerned look on his face. He asked if I was alright and if there was anything he could do. By that time, I had calmed down enough to talk with him without bursting into tears. I explained that I had no clue what was wrong with Dr. Zachery. It seemed to me he had gotten upset for no apparent reason that I could explain. The only thing I could remember doing is leaving the office to take my break and when I returned, all hell broke loose.

Dr. Levi indicated that he had never known Dr. Zachery to act in such an unprofessional manner before, but he would do his best to get to the bottom of this outburst. He further stated he planned to talk with Dr. Zachery and try to straighten this situation out as soon as possible. He apologized to me for all the trauma and said he hoped I would be okay. I knew it wasn't Dr. Levi's fault, and he had nothing to apologize for. In my opinion, the only person who needed to apologize was Dr. Zachery.

The time was growing late, and I knew my husband would soon come to pick me up from school. I tried to collect myself so I could go down stairs to meet him. I knew it was only a matter of minutes before he was due to arrive. I know I looked like a wreck. I tried to dry my eyes and compose myself so he would not know how upset I was. Dr. Carlson thought I should refrain from telling my husband what had happened because it might upset him too much. I agreed with his recommendation because I didn't want him upset either. I finally got myself together enough to go down to meet him, but I ran right into him as he was coming upstairs to find me.

When he looked at my face he immediately said, "What is wrong, Taffnee? You look like you've been crying."

Well, my first thought was to say nothing was wrong and try to brush the whole incident out of my mind, but instead, I said, "Oh, it was nothing."

Marcell insisted that I tell him what happened. I broke down and started to cry again as I told him about my encounter with Dr. Zachery. He grabbed my hand and said, "Come on, we're going back to that office right now. I won't have no man treating you that way and making you cry."

As we turned around to go back upstairs, I could tell Marcell was very agitated. I was afraid of his reaction once he saw Dr. Zachery. I knew he was not going to allow any man – much less a White man – to mistreat me.

When we returned to the office, Dr. Levi and Dr. Zachery were both sitting down at their desks. Dr. Zachery appeared to be working and he looked up as we entered the office door. My husband immediately said to Dr. Zachery, "Why are you threatening my wife? I don't appreciate you talking to my wife and threatening her the way you did and making her cry. You must be some kind of punk picking on a defenseless woman that way. I will kick your butt if you ever talk to my wife disrespectfully again!" Of course, you know Marcell was yelling by this time. "I bet you wouldn't talk to a man the way you talked to my wife! I won't have any man disrespecting her and making her cry! If you want someone to fight, then you will have to fight me instead of her. You must be some kind of real nut to pick on a woman the way you did."

Dr. Zachery stood up to address my husband's charges. "You don't know what happened. You don't understand." He looked a little intimidated as my husband moved closer to him. Dr. Zachery said, "I'll get the school security to get both of you out of my office if you come any closer!" Then he added, "I'm not afraid of you!"

I think my husband became so enraged over his cavalier attitude that he lunged for Dr. Zachery. By this time Dr. Levi had come around to the front of his desk and both of us grabbed my husband.

Dr. Zachery jumped back and said "I'll call security!"

Marcell didn't care. "Call security you punk, because I will never allow any man to mistreat my wife and make her cry the way you did. I don't know what you say she did, nor do I care at this point. I won't allow any man to insult, disrespect, or demean her in any way. I know you wouldn't allow me to talk to your wife the way you spoke to mine, no matter what she did."

Honestly, I don't know whether or not Dr. Zachery had a wife, but I know he got the point. I truly felt vindicated. I thought my husband looked so handsome and brave as he stood up to the bully professor who had not given me a reasonable explanation for his sudden crazed attitude change. Both men were yelling loudly, and Dr. Levi was trying to talk calmly to both men to try and defuse the situation. The hall started filling up again with other professors and students trying to figure out what was going on. Someone had run down the hall and gotten our friend, Dr. Carlson, to try and help control the situation.

Dr. Levi spoke calmly to Dr. Zachery and Dr. Carlson spoke calmly to Marcell, both trying to ease the situation before it turned into a brawl. Dr. Zachery did not say anything else to my husband, but backed up and began to move away. My husband told him, "You better not ever speak to my wife in that manner again or you'll have to answer directly to me."

Needless to say, I felt embarrassed, frightened, upset, and vindicated all at the same time. I could not for the life of me understand what had happened to Dr. Zachery to make him act the way he did. I tried to think what I could have done to make him go ballistic, but I had no clue. I thought maybe the man had a mental problem, or maybe he just didn't like Black people...or women. I didn't know anything about him personally, so I really had no basis from which to draw any conclusions about his behavior.

As I watched the situation continue to unfold, Dr. Zachery seemed to have lost some of the fierceness and anger that had been directed at me. He even looked frightened at the prospect that my husband wasn't afraid of him and seemed willing to fight him for insulting me. I certainly did not want my husband to get into any trouble, nor did I want to cause Dr. Levi or Dr. Carlson any trouble either. But I did not want to be subjected to any man who felt he could intimidate me and physically handle me without provocation.

Although I was happy that this apparent bully was getting what he deserved, I didn't want my husband to get into any trouble trying to defend me. I understood Marcell's anger, because I was angry too. However, I felt Dr. Zachery understood he could not threaten me without serious repercussions. I didn't want this unfortunate event to tarnish the rest of my time at the university. I didn't want it to negatively impact my work relationship with Dr. Levi. I just wanted the whole thing to be over.

I quickly gathered my books and other personal items from my desk and Marcell and I left the office with Dr. Carlson and Dr. Levi in tow. They both wanted to make sure I was okay. I assured them I was fine, and when I got home I would have a chance to relax and try to forget the unpleasant events of the day.

Dr. Levi asked, "Taffnee, will I see you tomorrow?"

"Yes," I answered. "Dr. Levi, please don't feel bad because you've done nothing wrong. I don't think I will have any more trouble out of Dr. Zachery. I think Marcell has made it very clear he can no longer intimidate me." I then turned to thanked Dr. Carlson for all his help and Marcell and I quickly walked down the stairs to find our car in the parking lot.

As we drove home, I said to Marcell, "I still don't understand what happened. I've never done anything to that guy, and for him to go off on me like that is so crazy." Marcell agreed. The rest of our evening was quiet and uneventful, but I was anxious and apprehensive about what the next day might bring. All I wanted to do was put this unpleasant episode behind me and finish out the rest of the quarter without incident.

When I spoke to Dr. Levi the next day, we decided it would be better if I avoided any contact with Dr. Zachery. I agreed this was probably the best course of action, and I would certainly do my part to make it work. Dr. Zachery and I never spoke again, thus avoiding any confrontation.

I have never been one to hold a grudge, and I pride myself on being a very forgiving person. After this incident, Dr. Levi made sure that Dr. Zachery was out of the office when I was scheduled to work. Conversely, if I arrived before he had a chance to leave the office, I would wait until he left before I entered the room. This plan seemed to work very well for everybody.

As time has a way of doing, it passes before you know it. I soon graduated from the University and put this awful experience behind me. I would often go back through the scenario in my mind trying to figure out why this whole thing happened the way it did, but I couldn't come up with any reasonable answers. Once I left the university, I never thought too much about Dr. Angus Zachery again, but occasionally I would reflect back on the situation trying to understand what really happened. I couldn't explain it, no matter how hard I tried. I knew Dr. Zachery was wrong, but it was going to take someone bigger than me to show him the error of his ways. I guess I thought it was one of those things God would have to reveal in His own time.

Several years had passed since I was a student at the University of South Florida. Marcell and I left St. Petersburg in 1979, relocating to Tallahassee, Florida after completing my Bachelor's Degree. I subsequently obtained my Master's Degree in Public Administration from Florida State University. Then, by 1982, my husband and I were living in Pensacola, Florida. We had jobs, a home, and had started a family. No matter where we lived, I made friends very easily. I always tried to be helpful in every situation I encountered. We became very entrenched in our community and established ourselves as hard workers and community-minded people with good Christian values. It didn't take me long to find some new friends and quickly get involved with whatever was going on.

Marcell and I had been living in Pensacola for a number of years when I started a weekly prayer service at my church. During this period of time I would ride the City bus to get to my destination. I had the opportunity to befriend a number of the bus drivers as I journeyed throughout the City. On this particular Tuesday morning I caught the bus as usual headed for prayer meeting. The bus driver and I started carrying on our usual conversation about everything and about nothing. I not only knew many of the drivers on a first name basis, but I was also very familiar with many of the bus routes around the City because I had occasion to travel many of them.

Since I rode the same bus every Tuesday morning, I became very friendly with the driver who drove the route. We laughed and talked extensively as I rode to my destination. As he pulled up to the next stop to pick up a passenger, a lady boarded the bus. She told him she was trying to get to a certain place that was supposed to be on his route. The driver told her, "This bus does not go near that location. The best thing for you to do is to return to the Transfer Station and catch a different bus that will get you closer to where you want to go. I will give you a transfer so you can catch the next bus back to the transfer station and get on the right bus."

The lady did not appear to be satisfied with his answer. She began to argue with the driver. "I called the transfer station before I left home and the dispatcher told me what bus I needed to catch. I just need to know where to get off to find my destination."

The driver then said, "You can stay on this bus, but I won't be going near where you want to go." He asked the lady to take a seat.

In a huff, she sat down next to me. She then said to the driver, "I spoke to the dispatcher and y'all need to get it together."

Feeling that the situation was getting out of hand between the passenger and the bus driver, I said to the lady with a big smile, "Excuse me." She then turned and looked in my direction. I continued, "I know exactly where you're going. You can ride this bus down to the next corner and walk a few blocks and then catch another bus that will take you right where you want to go. I go by there all the time and you don't have to go back to the transfer station to get there." The lady smiled and then thanked me and asked the driver to let her off at the next stop. I wasn't sure, but I assumed she was going to take my advice so she could continue her travels to her destination.

I was feeling pretty good because I felt like I had been a good friend to the driver and a good citizen at the same time. As I continued riding to my destination; sitting in the front seat where I usually sat talking to the driver, the bus driver suddenly said to me, "You obviously don't think I know my job?"

I said, "Excuse me. What do you mean?"

He said in a calm voice, "You think you know my job better than I do?"

I laughed nervously and said, "Of course not. I was only trying to be helpful. The lady wasn't happy with what you were saying."

"I've been doing this job for over 10 years and I have been trained to handle situations such as the one with that passenger. I know my job and I know what bus will get her to her destination in the most expedient manner." All of a sudden I experienced a flash back to 1978 when I had the big fight with Dr. Angus Zachery so many years ago.

As my thoughts moved back to the present, I heard the bus driver say, "You are undermining my authority with the customer and making it appear that I don't know my job." His comment fully explained what I had missed so many years ago in the altercation with Dr. Zachery.
"Wow!" I thought to myself, "Is that what I did? Is that why Dr. Zachery got so upset? Did he think I improperly interjected in his conversation with his student? Oh my God! Was I wrong then as I

Debra A. K. Thompson

am now?" Feeling embarrassed, I immediately apologized to the driver for interfering with his job and causing the passenger to question his knowledge and authority. I certainly thought I was right, but I finally realized I was dead wrong.

This situation, although simple in its development, caused me to do a lot of introspection and soul searching. It made me rethink my part in the blow-up that had occurred between me and Dr. Zachery so many years ago. The feeling that came over me was almost indescribable, and it made me feel like it was 1978 all over again. I could visualize myself back in the office as a student with Dr. Zachery. Now I understood his frustration and angst over what I had done --- I had undermined his authority. I became fully enlightened about the whole situation. It was crystal clear to me now what the real problem was...It was me!

Thankfully, the outcome in this instance was different from the outcome back in the office. I think the bus driver, unlike Dr. Zachery, spoke to me calmly and rationally. He pointed out my error in judgment in a logical and succinct manner. He forced me to understand my behavior for what it really was – not what I thought it was.

I had intended to be helpful, not harmful. But with all my good intentions, I was out of order. Upon further examination, it made me realize that maybe, just maybe, the whole thing was not all Dr. Zachery's fault as I had so proudly concluded in my innocence back in 1978. Maybe, just maybe, I had some blame to bear for the whole incident. Obviously, I missed the point of the lesson until that time.

One thing I am sure of is that Dr. Zachery did not handle his part of this whole situation with the professionalism he probably desired, nor did I handle my part of the situation with the common sense it deserved. I handled myself as a 22-year-old with 22-year-

68

old logic, but I realized, when I looked back at that moment, that I had undermined his authority in front of his student. I think his reaction was "over-the-top" and exaggerated, but I don't think he knew what else to do.

As I think back on the entire incident, I realize that Dr. Zachery was just a young guy who probably had been teaching for a few years and he did not need or want a student interjecting with advice to his other students. Moreover, he probably never encountered a situation like that one. Conversely, the bus driver being a more mature person probably realized I did not mean any harm, but used this opportunity as a teaching moment for me.

In every situation there is a lesson that can be learned. Sometimes we think we are right in the position we hold, but we are clearly wrong. At the time, no one could have explained what I did wrong because I genuinely believed I was right. As I think back on the events of that day, I recognize I was an interfering know-it-all. I was under the false assumption that just because I thought I knew a thing, it meant I should share it…even if I wasn't asked.

There is an old adage that says: "The hardest person to convince they are wrong is the one who thinks he is right." I truly thought I was right, and it took me many years and another similar incident to finally help me correct my behavior. I fully realized at that moment how wrong I was.

I always thought it was my job to be helpful. I thought I was being helpful to a fellow student when that clearly wasn't my job. I also thought I was being helpful to a fellow passenger on the bus - and that wasn't my job either. For years, I convinced myself that I bore no fault in the altercation with Dr. Zachery and it was entirely his fault for carrying on like a maniac without an explanation. However, I realize now I wouldn't have accepted any responsibility at that time. I think his "over-the-top" behavior only worked to reinforce my belief that he was wrong and I was right.

As I continue to reflect back on my behavior, I now see that I had a terrible habit of interfering in situations that did not require my input. Every situation we encounter in life has lessons that we are supposed to learn. Sometimes it takes us years of repeating the same behavior before the light finally comes on.

As I now know, and you need to know, when you don't learn a lesson the first time, you are doomed to repeat it until the lesson is finally learned. I was thankful I had the opportunity to apologize to the bus driver for my interference in his job. However, I wasn't sure if I would ever have the opportunity to see Dr. Zachery again to make amends.

That's why it was so amazing when, one day while visiting my parents, I happened to be channel surfing when I saw Dr. Angus Zachery on television. He was still teaching at the University. It was obvious from his conversation he had become very prominent in his field of study. He was on a show with another professor, and they were talking about a subject that I can't even remember.

A strange feeling came over me and I felt compelled to contact him. I pondered in my mind whether or not I should reach out to him. My first thoughts were: "What if he remembers me and hangs up the phone? What if he doesn't remember me at all and hangs up the phone? What would I say to him after all these years? Would he even be interested in hearing what I had to say?"

Although I hadn't seen Dr. Zachery in well over 20 years, he was still very recognizable.
His hair was a little thinner on the top and his physique was a little heavier, but I immediately knew who he was. During the show, his contact information was posted, so I sprang into action to get the

number. To my surprise, it wasn't very difficult to reach his office. The receptionist on duty let me know he was on a sabbatical for the semester, but I could probably catch him at home. I felt a little hesitant to call his home, but I felt this was something important I needed to do.

It's amazing how God can orchestrate a seemingly impossible situation to help you do what needs to be done. Once I dialed the number, I started having reservations about calling him. I didn't want to re-ignite long since forgotten emotions or create any problems. However, I knew I had to call and apologize.

It didn't matter to me whether or not he remembered me; it only mattered that I remembered him. I knew I owed him an apology for my past behavior, even if he didn't remember all the details of what had happened. I remembered it just like it was yesterday. I didn't see how he could have forgotten such a horrific event, but it was certainly possible. At this juncture, I only knew I had to apologize and let him know I understood his position.

I finally worked up the nerve to call him at home. I wasn't sure how I would start or what I would say, but I figured if he answered the phone I would say something. As the phone began to ring, fear swept over my body.

How would I begin the conversation? Would he be willing to listen to me after all these years? Would he even remember me or even care? I didn't know the answer to any of these questions, but I had to try. I wasn't sure what I was going to say, but when he answered the phone and said, "Hello?" I just started talking.

"Hello. Dr. Zachery you may not remember me, but my name is Taffnee Johnson and I use to be an intern for Dr. Levi back in the late 70's. Do you remember when you and Dr. Levi shared an office?"

"Yes I do." To my surprise he had a very pleasant sounding voice and was quite friendly. Not at all like what I remembered.

"Well, I am calling to apologize to you for the big fight we had way back in 1978."

With a surprised tone to his voice he said, "We had a fight?" I wanted to believe he really remembered, but I think he wanted to hear what I had to say. As I began to recount the story to him, he laughed nervously and then said, "I can't believe I would have behaved that way!" Then he asked, "Are you sure it was me?"

"Oh yes, I am absolutely sure it was you."

"I can't believe I would have acted in such a horrible manner." He didn't deny my claim, but he didn't confirm it either. He kept laughing and repeating, "I can't believe you are talking about me." He seemed very amused as I recounted the facts of the story. Finally, he said, "If I acted like that, Taffnee, I want to apologize to you. I really can't believe I would have carried on that way."

"I know it sounds funny now, but at the time it was anything *but* funny. However, I owe *you* an apology, not the other way around."

Dr. Zachery sounded confused. "If I behaved like that, why do you owe me an apology?"

"Well," I explained, "I had a recent incident happen in my life that helped me understand the whole unpleasant episode with more clarity. For a long time, I thought it was you who was wrong and I was the innocent party. I always felt it was you who owed me an apology, but God has shown me my shortcomings and how my meddling, although well intended, was out of place."

I continued, "I now understand I should never have interfered with your duties as a teacher and advisor to another student by interjecting my unsolicited advice into your conversation." I hesitated a moment and then said, with a little tongue-in-cheek, "I do think you over-reacted just a little, but I understand and appreciate your position. It took me a lot of years to realize it had nothing to do with me being Black or female, as I had originally concluded, but it was all about me being a meddling student."

I am sure Dr. Zachery had placed that incident so far out of his mind just like I did, but he never denied it happened. I know it had been a long time, but I felt he didn't want to make it any worse than it had been at that time. I am sure he wanted it to be forgotten and buried with the past never to be resurrected again, but I find God has a way of giving us a chance to make things right if we will just do it. I think my apology not only freed me, but it freed him as well.

He replied, "Thank you for calling, but you really didn't have to do that. I still can't believe I would have acted that way. That would have been so unprofessional and not at all like me."

I laughed and then said, "It's okay, because I don't believe I should have acted that way either." I let him know how appreciative I was that he took my call and allowed me a chance to apologize.

Our conversation then switched from apologies to sharing news. "Did you know Dr. Levi had passed away?" he asked.

"Yes, Dr. Carlson told me."
His tone was surprised again. "You mean Timothy Carlson?"

"Yes, Dr. Carlson and I have remained friends throughout the years and he always keeps me abreast about things happening at the university."

"Didn't he retire?"

"Yes, but he still lives in the St. Petersburg area." Our conversation had changed, and now we were talking like equals, and I felt good to be able to share information with him.

"I didn't know what happened to him once he retired," he said, a little wistfully. "So many of the people from that era have retired or passed away. It's good to know Timothy is doing well."

Although I called Dr. Zachery to apologize, our conversation shifted and we began to talk like old friends. As we concluded our talk, it was obvious to me he wasn't the raging ogre I remembered from so many years ago. I found his conversation quite engaging and noted that we had many friends in common as we began to discuss mutual acquaintances and current events happening at the university.

I thanked Dr. Zachery again for being so nice and taking my call. I told him that I knew he didn't have to speak to me at all, but that I was so glad he did. Graciously he said, "I appreciate you calling because you didn't have to call me, either, and I thank you, too."

We exchanged a few more pleasantries and said our goodbyes. After we hung up, I felt a hundred-pound weight had been lifted from my chest. It made me feel good to finally close that chapter of my life with Dr. Zachery. I realized it wasn't about him at all, but it was all about me. This incident wasn't something I thought of very often, but there were times it came back to my mind unconsciously. If I had not had the encounter with the bus driver that day, I probably would have gone through the rest of my life blaming Dr. Zachery for the whole unpleasant episode without understanding my contribution.

I am now able to look at myself and my behavior in a more objective manner. I think this situation helped me to make course corrections before other negative things happened. I never thought of myself as an interfering person; only a helpful person. I have found in most instances that people only appreciate your help when they ask for it. Unsolicited help is far less appreciated, and more likely than not to be rejected or ignored. I think God was trying to give me a wake-up call so that I could learn something about myself, and become a better person at the same time.

I couldn't see it then, but I now know the whole point of this lesson was to teach me respect and forgiveness: respect for others as well as myself and learning to forgive and ask for forgiveness.

How often are we wrong, but we fail to take time to acknowledge it and make corrections? Some lessons take a little bit longer to learn than others, but the important thing is to learn it before it is too late. I may never have the opportunity to speak to Dr. Zachery again, but I am so glad God gave me the presence of mind to do it and make amends before it was too late. However, the most important thing I learned from this situation was to "stay in my own lane."

Debra A. K. Thompson

PART IV

A Songwriter Is Born

As I reflect back over my childhood, I realize now that I have always loved to write and sing. Ever since I was a little girl, I have always wanted to play the piano. However, like most young children, I had a desire, but was unwilling to do the things I needed to do to become better, like practicing.

My sisters and I enjoyed singing together, which started when we were very young. My grandmother would teach us three older children cute little church songs and let us sing them on Sunday evenings during the Baptist Training Union program (BTU.) She taught us songs like, "He's Got the Whole World in His Hands," "A New Created World," and "Faith, Hope and Charity," along with many other popular songs being sung at that time.

As a matter of fact, my whole family was a musical family. My mom had a beautiful voice, and my dad could sing as well. My dad was very shy when it came to any public display of talent, but there was no shortage of talent when it came to singing at home or in the car. My dad always taught us little fun songs that we could sing together and all of us girls loved to back him up. One of my favorite songs we sang with him was, "The Green Grass."

I loved to sing all types of songs, but I especially loved opera music. I thought I might one day become an opera singer. Therefore, it wasn't strange that when I grew up and had children of my own, I always had music and singing around the house.

Although my life had moved in a different direction from my youthful desire of becoming an opera singer, I always kept a close association with music through the church. I grew up singing in the church choir, and on several occasions even directed the youth choir. Additionally, I worked with a couple of community choirs which only strengthened my love and desire for music.

Things like that came naturally to me, and it didn't seem like a chore to prepare myself to work on the music. I was always an avid reader, and I like creating my own stories, so it didn't seem strange to me that I toyed around with the words of songs - arranging and rearranging them.

I would experiment with different tempos to see how that would impact the sound of the song as well. I think somewhere deep down inside I had aspirations of one day becoming a writer of some kind. However, as I grew into adulthood, many of my youthful tendencies took a back seat to reality. Whether or not my gift for writing stories, songs, or even poetry would continue to flourish was something I had to discover later in life.

After graduating from college with my Master's Degree, my husband Marcell and I moved to the Pensacola, Florida area. My first job was at the Naval Air Rework Facility (NARF.) I was one of four people who worked in my section, along with a supervisor, and we were responsible for ensuring all the command manuals stayed up to date with the latest regulations. My position was an entry-level position as a Management Assistant.

The job was not a difficult one because I was doing something I already enjoyed doing- reading and writing. I had to update old command policy manuals with the latest revision of the policy. I also had to review draft regulations and identify any grammatical or sentence structure errors that might exist before final publication. My co-workers were nice and we all got along fairly well.

One day while I was sitting at my desk, I didn't have a lot of work to do, so I decided to do some writing on my own. I started writing down words of some old familiar songs on a pad of paper. I am not even sure why I started to write the words down, but I began to study the words and look at how each stanza was constructed.

I didn't have a song book of any kind at my desk for guidance, so I placed the punctuation and words the way I would normally sing them. I felt very proud of myself for doing so. I did not want anyone to see what I was writing because it wasn't part of my work routine. However, my co-worker, Fred Epson came up from behind me and got a glimpse of some of the words I had written on the pad.

He said, "I read some of the words on your paper, Taffnee, and those are some beautiful words. Is this a song or a poem?"

"This is a song," I replied.

"Did you write this?"

"No, this is an old familiar hymn we sing at our church." I paused, then continued, "I have tried to write a few original songs in the past, but I don't know how good they are. I just like the words of these particular songs, so I decided to write them down. I do like to try my hand at a little poetry and storytelling every now and then."

"I write songs myself and sometimes I doodle around with words on paper like you are doing," Fred admitted, then added, "I mostly write country songs."

"Have you ever had any of your songs published, Fred?" I asked, genuinely interested.

"Yes. I even have several of my songs being sung by a couple of local groups."

I was impressed. "That's really good."

"Good songs can be very valuable, especially if they are accepted by someone famous."

"I've never shown anybody my songs because I never thought any of them were good enough to share. I mostly write poems, stories, and rearrange other people's songs for the choir I direct." I was starting to feel a little embarrassed.

"Seems like you have a good eye for good words." Fred smiled, then walked away.

I mumbled, "Thank you," and then put my pad away in my desk and got back to work. I didn't intend for anyone to see what I was writing, but since Fred saw what I was doing, it gave me encouragement to keep working on my music. I think he recognized the gift within me.

I believe that was the first time I thought seriously about working more on my own songs. I don't know why his comments seemed to resonate with me somewhere in my spirit, but I found myself thinking I might have the needed skills to write a good song. I wasn't sure if I had what it took to be a serious song writer, but I thought it might be worth my time to see if it was something I could really do. The one thing I had going for me was that I did know a good song when I heard one.

During the early- to mid-80's, it seemed to me that the music being played on the radio and being sung in many churches during that time was not very original. Most of the songs were re-makes of old songs with a different arrangement. I thought to myself, "If these people can take an old song and rearrange it, thereby creating a new flavor, why couldn't I do the same?"

Although I didn't fully realize it at the time, Fred's comments made me think seriously about my own writing skills and where it could potentially go if I devoted myself to the endeavor. Consequently, I started writing down more words of songs I liked and comparing them to the original words of songs I had written.

I would arrange and rearrange the words as needed to get the affect I desired. I think this was a way for me to improve my writing by working with already established songs other people had written. It gave me an opportunity to try to change my own songs without any fear of rejection or judgment.

As I think back now, I can remember there were many times in my life when I had dreams about music and songs. In a lot of those dreams I could hear words that would inspire and lift me up. I assumed other people had similar dreams just like I did. I never shared many of these dreams with others because I took them as just dreams; nothing really important. I didn't understand the true value of what was happening to me. I always enjoyed the dreams, but I didn't do anything about them, nor did I know if there was anything I should be doing about them.

These types of dreams went on for many years. Sometimes I would hear the most beautiful singing and music I had ever heard in my life. However, when I would awaken in the morning I knew I had heard a beautiful song in my sleep, but I usually never remembered any of the words.

I now realize that God was giving me something special, but I valued my sleep more. I would always say to myself, "If I dream about another song, I'm going to get up and write the words down." Of course, that never happened. I was pretty lazy when it came to getting up in the middle of the night. I lost many a song because I wouldn't obey that voice deep down in my spirit urging me to get up and write it down.

Sometimes the songs would be so good that I would tell my husband about them in the morning, but I could never remember the tune or any of the words. It was wonderful to have such beautiful dreams, but it was also frustrating not to remember anything in the morning. To hear such beautiful songs in the middle of the night; yet be too lazy to get up and write them down, was a challenge I found difficult to overcome. I know God had to be pretty frustrated with me. He was constantly trying to give me something good, but I could not understand why He would not allow me to remember all the good stuff He gave me throughout the night.

On numerous occasions throughout my childhood and adulthood, I took lots of piano lessons. I thought that if I learned how to play it might help me with my vocal and songwriting skills. I always enjoyed the lessons, but I was like so many piano students...I didn't want to practice. I would take lessons for a while and then stop for a while. I never stuck with it long enough to become proficient, but I got enough to learn some of the basics. That's why I was so excited when I found out my son Daniels's day care would be offering piano lessons to the children.

My son Daniel seemed genuinely excited about taking piano lessons. I hoped he would do something I had failed to do in all my years of taking lessons - actually learn how to play. His first piano teacher was Judy Brazelton. She was a young female with pretty blue eyes and blonde hair. She had a very thin build with a beautiful smile. There were about five or six other kids in the class, and they all appeared to be excited about being in the class as well. At the first recital, they learned to play some simple little songs appropriate for their age group. However, when the summer came the class was discontinued due to lack of enrollment.

I felt hopeful the class would be reinstated and more children would enroll after the summer vacation was over, but some of the original students did not return after summer break. I was very disappointed to learn they could not get enough children to start a new class; therefore, it was dropped from the schedule. I think there were only two other children besides Daniel who signed up to take the piano class, and they needed a minimum of six children for a teacher to be assigned. I was happy when Daniel told me he wanted to continue his music lessons anyway, so I asked Judy if she would be willing to give him private lessons. She agreed to come to our home and teach him.

Judy and I established a great rapport with one another. She worked well with Daniel and he was learning rapidly. Daniel seemed to like the lessons a lot, and he looked forward to them each week. I told Judy how I had taken piano lessons many times through the years, but had never learned the fundamentals well enough to play any songs other than the simple ones I was taught to play. Judy thought she could teach me some basics that would help me learn to play more songs if I wanted to take some lessons from her. I told her I would be glad to take lessons from her and maybe this time I would stick with it long enough to learn some good technique. I thought this would also do a couple of things: One, help me to learn how to play more songs, and two, encourage Daniel and me to practice. In my estimation this was a win/win situation for everybody.

Daniel and I took lessons from Judy for approximately one year. In that time, I learned a lot of techniques I had not learned during previous lessons. I don't know if we were the best students she ever had, but we were faithful and enthusiastic. I thought I was finally going to get to be a pretty good musician, until one day she stopped by the house and said, "I am going to have to discontinue our lessons. I am getting married in a couple of months and I will be moving away. I've got to prepare for the wedding and prepare to move as well, so I won't be able to continue our lessons."

The news caught me off guard because I wasn't aware she was even engaged. I told her, "I understand. I am really excited for you and I will miss you a whole lot. Do you know anyone who can continue to give Daniel and me lessons? I've gotten very spoiled with you coming to the house, and I sure would like to get someone else who could do the same."

"I really don't know anybody, but I'll check with a few of my friends who give piano lessons and see if I can find someone." Well, I assume she got busy with her wedding plans and forgot all about us. There I was again, only learning enough to be dangerous, but not really good.

I started asking people around my job if they knew any good piano teachers who would give lessons at home. I got several recommendations, but one name kept coming up in my conversations...Mr. Sam Williams. I did not know Mr. Sam personally, but I had heard very good things about him. I decided to give him a call and get more information.

He sounded very nice over the phone, so we set up a date to meet. He was a big, husky man...tall with a very healthy build. He had a receding hair line and he wore glasses. He reminded me of a nice big talented teddy bear. He had a very easy-going manner and was very soft spoken. I liked Mr. Sam from the first time we met and I found we had several friends in common. The main thing was to ensure my son liked him too. Needless to say, Daniel seemed to like him so we set it up to start lessons with him on the next week.

Daniel and I started out taking lessons from Mr. Sam and pretty soon my youngest son, Caleb, and my husband, Marcell, wanted to take lessons also. Before long all four of us were taking lessons from Mr. Sam at the same time. It was a lot of fun to have the entire family participating in such a positive activity. Unfortunately, Marcell didn't stick with the lessons very long, but the boys and I enjoyed the lessons so much we opted to continue a while longer. I was very hopeful this was the start of a long association that might net me a real music and songwriting career if I truly devoted myself to the endeavor.

Well, the years kept passing and I kept working on my songwriting skills, but not moving forward in any substantive way. I still had a desire to write. So, when I was approached with an opportunity to do some free-lance writing for a local Christian-based magazine called, "Gospel Express," this had me very excited!

The magazine was started by a young military guy by the name of S. Q. Morton. I knew I had a gift for writing, but I thought I needed a more structured opportunity to demonstrate my talents and build my confidence. That's what I believe S. Q. gave me – a chance to prove myself. I started out by writing short inspirational articles and then moved to full-featured interview stories. Some people might say I got "lucky," but I know this was God's way of directing me to the things He ultimately wanted me to do.

As I think back, I now realize S. Q. gave me more than just a writing opportunity; he gave me a growth opportunity too. Since I wasn't very confident in my own writing abilities, this was a safe way to test my writing skills in a secure environment. It also gave me real-world experience. He provided exposure to many of the things I needed to enhance my gift as a writer. Even though I never received monetary compensation for the stories I wrote, I received lots of exposure and public recognition. I know I am a better person – and a better writer – because of my time at the Gospel Express Magazine.

By the mid 90's, I had been doing a lot of writing for the Gospel Express Magazine. I had become an integral part of the day-to-day operation of the publication. Consequently, it wasn't a surprise to me when S. Q. asked me to take over the position as director, editor, and publisher of the magazine. He had received transfer orders to another duty station and he didn't want the magazine to close. I enjoyed the work so much that I decided to accept the responsibility of this challenge.

The plan was to maintain the magazine until he returned to

Pensacola in a couple of years. I held the position for approximately three years and learned a lot about the publishing business. After it became clear S. Q. wasn't going to return to the Pensacola area anytime soon, I transferred my responsibilities to a young man by the name of Larry Irving. I am very thankful for the opportunity S. Q. gave me. It helped me to develop some much-needed skills I would utilize in my work as a songwriter in the future. As much as I loved working there, it was more than I could handle with my current duties as a wife and mother.

Although I loved to write articles and stories, somewhere in my subconscious mind I knew songwriting was a part of my future as well. I wasn't sure when, or if, I would ever see the results of the music I felt deep down in my heart, but it was nice to think about. I realize, now, that God was grooming me for the work He wanted me to do, but I did not always recognize the signs as He sent them. I soon relinquished my responsibilities with the magazine, but I kept myself busy with my writing and music lessons.

Since I was a little more advanced in my music skills than my sons were, I wanted to learn something a little bit different from the lessons they would receive. I expressed to Mr. Sam that I had taken traditional piano lessons many times in the past, but I wanted to learn how to play by "ear". Mr. Sam said he could teach me the basics and help me understand the fundamentals of the music. I thought if I could learn to play by "ear" I might have a chance of learning how to play some popular songs – maybe even some of the songs I wrote myself.

At this point in my life, I had not had a musical dream for quite a while. Consequently, it was a big surprise to me when one night I dreamed about a song in my sleep. As usual, I did not get up to write anything down because I thought I would remember it in the morning. It was a beautiful song. It sounded like the angels were singing to me and I woke up the next morning singing it.

Unlike all the other times I heard singing in my sleep this time I was actually able to remember the words and the melody of the song. Needless to say, I was so excited to wake up and actually remember something. I jumped up and ran to the piano to try and play it. To my surprise, praise God, I was able to put together a few chords and pick out the melody of the song on the piano. Nothing like this had ever happened to me before and it was very exciting to think I finally remembered a song God was giving me.

I could hardly wait until Mr. Sam got to the house for our piano lessons later in the week. I thought to myself, "Boy is he going to be surprised at what I can do!" When the day finally arrived for our lesson, I told Mr. Sam, "I wrote another song! I heard it in my sleep and I've been working on it so I could show you what it sounds like."

Mr. Sam replied, "That sounds great!! Can you play it or sing it for me?"

"Absolutely!" I said. I started playing and singing my song, "*I was glad when they said unto me, I was glad when they said unto me, I was glad when they said unto me: let us go into the house of the Lord.*" When I finished, I said proudly, "This was taken from Psalm 122, and God gave me the tune."

Mr. Sam looked at me with that serious facial expression he sometimes displayed and said, "You wrote that?"

I said, "Yes" with such pride and excitement. "I know the words are from the Bible, but the melody is mine…What do you think?"

"Well, it's very nice, but are you sure you wrote that?" I thought I detected a little doubt in Mr. Sam's tone, but I was so excited about my accomplishment I put it out of my mind.

"Yes I did!! God gave me this song in my sleep. I know it came from Him because it's coming directly from a scripture."

Although he still sounded a little reticent, I just thought he was impressed because it sounded so good. Mr. Sam said, "Ok, that's very nice."

Well, I sort of felt like he didn't believe I could write a song that good, and maybe that's why he sounded so skeptical. However, his skepticism didn't diminish my enthusiasm one bit. I felt proud because I could play and sing a song I had written myself. I asked Mr. Sam, "Can you show me a few more chords I can use to make my song sound even better?"

"Yes" he said. He then showed me a few extra chords to help me make it sound a little fuller and I was off and running. I played it for my husband and my children when they came home. I was proud of myself and I think they were proud of me too.

I think the experience of writing something I felt was very good and also original ignited a thirst in me to write more songs and learn how to play them. I didn't have any new songs I thought I could play, but I started working hard on learning songs I already knew and decided to perfect the one song God had given me in my sleep. I felt so proud of myself that I began to practice this song every day to try and play it better and better. I thought if I practiced hard enough this song could possibly become a hit. I wanted to play it well enough to present it to others who could then learn it and sing along as I played. Wow, what an awesome thought…Me, a real songwriter! A real musician!

After that experience, I prayed and asked God to give me more songs. I promised Him I would be faithful and write the words down no matter what time He gave them to me. I promised Him I would really do it this time and not let anything get in my way…like sleep. I am sure God knew in my heart I wanted to do just what I had said, but He also knew I probably wouldn't do it.

Thank God for His mercy and grace, because he started giving me words and melodies of songs only during the daytime. I would be at the park with my children and, all of a sudden, a song would pop into my head and I would have to rush the kids home so I could write it down. I then decided I needed to take a tape recorder with me to the park so I could not only capture the words, but I could record the melody as well. This felt very exciting to me. I thought I was finally becoming a real songwriter and musician. I could now pluck out a few little tunes that popped into my head and make them recognizable.

Time was steadily passing and I hadn't done anything significant with my song, "I Was Glad When They Said Unto Me," but I kept practicing it every chance I got. As usual, time kept on moving and a few years had gone by since I wrote that song. I had written several other songs in the interim, but I was most proud of that one.

One day as I was working around the house, I was listening to the radio and I heard a song being played that sounded vaguely familiar. I couldn't quite put my finger on it, but I knew I had heard it before. It was a hand-clapping, foot-stomping song. *"I was glad when they said unto me, I was glad when they said unto me, I was glad when they said unto me: let us go into the house of the Lord."* HMMM I thought to myself, "This song has a close similarity to my song." The words of course were the same words I had heard in my dream, but the tune was almost identical to mine.

This song was just a little bit faster than my song, but it was almost the same.

I couldn't believe it! How could anyone know my song? "This can't be happening to me!" I said out loud. "Somebody is singing my song! I just don't believe it! How could they know my song? I never shared it with anybody but Mr. Sam and my family."

"What am I going to do?" I thought to myself. "I'm going to call that radio station right now and find out who in the world is singing my song." It's amazing how indignant you feel when something like this happens. I knew I hadn't done anything with the song, but I had big plans – at least in my mind.

I hurriedly dialed the number to the station and the Gospel DJ answered the phone. "980 WRNE. Jimmy John speaking. How can I help you?"

Being a regular listener of the station during the week, I was pretty familiar with Jimmy John. I had spoken to him on a few occasions and I knew he could answer my question right away. I felt comfortable speaking to him about my issue. He listened patiently as I explained the reason for my call.

"You are playing my song!" I said in an excited tone.

"I am?" he answered with puzzlement in his voice. "What song are you talking about?"

"The song you are playing now: 'I Was Glad When They Said Unto Me.' Yes! I wrote that song!" I boasted.

"You did?"

"Yes, I did…several years ago."

"Ok, I didn't know that."

I then asked in a confused tone, "Who is singing my song? Who is this choir?"

"Let me look it up for you," he said. "I didn't know you wrote songs."

With a bit of pride in my voice, I replied, "Yes I do and this is one of my best!"

He said, "It looks like the Georgia Mass Choir is singing this song."

I asked him, "When was this album released?"

"Let me get the album cover and I'll check it for you…1979."

"1979?"

"Yes, 1979."

"Hmmm…" It had become painfully obvious that I had made a big mistake. I laughed out loud and then said to Jimmy John, "I guess maybe I didn't write it after all, huh?

He said, "I guess not." We both started laughing.

"Thank you very much, I'll talk with you later." As I slowly hung up the phone I couldn't imagine how I could have made such a huge mistake. I thought I wrote this song.

I guess you know I was totally embarrassed and felt like a complete fool. How could I think I could have written something so good?

Now it made sense to me why my piano teacher, Mr. Sam, had responded to me in the way he did earlier. It was because he had already heard the song and knew I couldn't have possibly written it. He was so kind and did not call me a liar, or discourage me from pursuing my newly-found passion as a songwriter, but he let me work hard and build on what I thought I had done.

Well, after the reality of my situation sank into my head, I knew I had to tell Mr. Sam of my discovery. I knew when he came over for our lesson I would need to take back my claim of writing "I Was Glad When They Said Unto Me." I thought it was kind of hilarious because I *really* thought I had written that song. Up until that point you couldn't have convinced me otherwise. I don't ever remember hearing it before that day so I had no reason to think I didn't write it.

It dawned on me that maybe God was trying to get my attention all the time, but the only way He could do it was to give me an already proven song that I could become excited about. It's not that He hadn't given me great songs in the past, but the times He was giving them to me required me to get out of my comfort zone to harvest the find.

The light finally came on in my head. I knew God had already gifted me as a writer, but I needed to work the gift. What God had been doing previously was giving me treasures that required me to do something in order to find the true value. I wanted Him to drop everything in my lap and all I wanted to do was pick it up and run with it. Now I realize how unwilling I was to do what needed to be done.

I found out that is not always the way God will give you something valuable. Sometimes He will give you a gift that requires very little effort to capitalize on its worth. It's not that He hadn't given me great songs in the past, but the times he was giving them to me required me to do some work to reap the benefits. I finally became enlightened enough to understand what I hadn't understood before.

I now know He sometimes gives us only the raw materials we need and we must cultivate the ground to reap the harvest.

When Mr. Sam came to the house for piano lessons later on that week, I immediately told him what had transpired earlier. With a giggle I said to Mr. Sam, "I heard my song being played on the radio. I found out it was recorded by the Georgia Mass choir back in the 70's. I guess you know I did not write the song, "I Was Glad When They Said unto Me." I guess you already knew that?"

With a big smile on his face, he said, "Well, I wasn't sure so I didn't want to say anything. I could have been wrong. I didn't want to discourage you because you were so excited."

I expressed my dismay at how I could have made such a huge mistake.

"Taffnee, I think there are times when God gives more than one person the same idea about a thing," he said, "but I think God allows the one who is willing to get up and do the work necessary to accomplish the mission to gain the credit."

I said, "I guess that is what happened to me. When God was trying to give me songs, I wasn't willing to get up from my sleep and write them down. So I guess He had to get my attention by giving me something already published. I honestly declare I never heard that song before that date, but maybe I heard it and forgot I heard it."

Mr. Sam said, "That is certainly possible, but I think the main thing is that you are now willing to do the work necessary to harvest the original songs God is giving you. You aren't the only one who has ever failed to recognize a gold mine when it's right in front of you. I think we go for the 'Fool's Gold' rather than digging for the real treasure."

I knew in my heart of hearts he was right. It didn't take a rocket scientist to finally figure out what God was trying to tell me all the time. It was simply a matter of willingness. I know now I was unwilling, not unable, to take advantage of what He wanted to give me. I know now God had given me many talents and abilities. Some of them came more naturally than others, but all of them required development.

Mr. Sam and I began laughing hysterically at the situation as this episode became our little private joke. I now understand why people say God has a good sense of humor because He sure got my attention! I couldn't do anything but appreciate His patience with me.

God could have easily removed the gifts he had given me and transferred them to somebody else who was more willing to pay attention. I realize now I was just like that man in Matthew 25: 15-28 who had been given one talent, but chose to bury it rather than use it. As a result, his talent was given to the man who had the most talent because he didn't make excuses; he made it happen.

As a result of what I thought was a calamity, God birthed the Gospel Songwriters Music Workshop through my obedience in 1994. This workshop is for others who are just like me: gifted, but afraid to use their gifts. Many times we don't capitalize on what we have because we are too afraid of failure, rejection, or discouragement from those who didn't give us the gifts in the first place. The focus of this lesson is to trust and believe that "All things work together for good to them that love God and are the called according to His purpose." (Romans 8:28.) It may not always be clear why things in life happen as they do, but instead I am learning how to trust that God knows what He is doing when He entrusted me with my abilities.

Now I am working diligently on the original songs God is giving me. I am not only writing more songs, but I am giving other songwriters the opportunity to benefit from my experience as an aspiring songwriter. Moreover, I also write articles for a few small publications that appreciate the information I have to share. The fact that I am able to tell my story in this book is a major accomplishment.

I think God is always waiting for us to realize He has given us everything we need to succeed, but it is up to us to do the work. We must learn how to make the right connections to make it happen. I am thankful to God for not getting tired of waiting on me to do what He wanted me to do. Instead, He gave me the opportunity to mature and finally recognize the great blessings I've been given.

Debra A. K. Thompson

PART V

All I Wanted Was Some Tile

Have you ever wanted something so badly that you could taste it, see it, smell it, and almost touch it, but you didn't know how in the world you were ever going to achieve it? I found myself in this position several times during this period of my life: trying to make things happen which seemed simple to do, but hard to accomplish.

I am thinking of the time when my husband and I bought our first home in the summer of 1984. I thought I had found the ideal place and I would never want another home again. However, as time goes by, you find other ways to make a good thing even better. I have found that even if you love the first place you ever purchased, you still want to make changes and improvements, no matter how good it seems at the beginning.

Well, that's where I found myself when I think about my first house. It was a very beautiful home and I felt very proud to have it. I knew from the first time I saw it that it was the house for me. At the time I was about five months pregnant and my husband, Marcell and I were looking for the perfect home to raise our family.

This house had everything I thought I wanted in a home and more...four bedrooms, 2 bathrooms, living room, family room, dining room, kitchen, etc. It was directly across the street from a neighborhood park and we had a nice fenced back yard for our children to enjoy. I don't think I could have asked for a more splendid place as a first-time home buyer.

By now I am sure you are saying to yourself, "This sounds very nice, but a lot of people buy houses every day. What makes this story important enough for you to share?" Well, I must say the story itself is not the most important thing, but the principles I learned through this process is what makes it all worth sharing. I have come to understand that even the smallest things in our lives have purpose and meaning if we are willing to embrace it.

I can remember everything like it was yesterday. When I first saw the house, I knew it was the right house for me. I felt excited and satisfied with our find and wanted nothing more than to move in and start living. I thought I loved everything about the house until we moved our personal items in.

It seems like in every good woman's life changes must be made whether they are needed or not. Time does bring about a change. Things that are great today sometimes become improvement projects of tomorrow. It doesn't mean there's anything wrong, but you just want something different.

At the time, I considered the things I wanted to do to the house as cosmetic changes. However, the one thing about having a spouse, partner, or significant other is that they have opinions too. Sometimes things that sound so simple to do such as, changing carpet, flooring, furniture, and window dressings can become a major undertaking. I knew these things would enhance the beauty of the house and make it more our own, but getting another person to see your vision can become a little tricky. It doesn't matter how simple a project may seem to you; it all comes back to money and taste in most instances in the end.

The first change we decided to make was to the carpet. The carpet was dark brown shag that probably looked great during the time it was installed, but did not fit the initial color scheme we were going for. The new carpet we chose was light brown low pile carpeting called "Clay Pot." It was easy to clean and could be matched with many different colors of furniture and curtains. That appeared to be an easy fix that we both could buy into.

The next thing we changed was the kitchen floor. The flooring was a brown and yellow vinyl and it looked good when we first saw it, but after living in the house for a few months it became too busy and colorful for our decor. The replacement flooring we chose was a white vinyl with specks of yellow-gold to bring out the color of the cabinets and the counter tops. Everything was going along just beautifully in my estimation.

I decided not to change the wallpaper in the kitchen and breakfast area because they coordinated perfectly with the new vinyl flooring we picked. In my opinion the colors we selected were the "absolute bomb" and I was very happy with our progress. I found some gorgeous white and brown curtains with a yellow and green ruffled fruit pattern that I thought would last in the kitchen for many years and give me the versatility I was after. I considered most of the things we did as basic improvements that made the house feel more like our home.

Our little family was off to a good start and there was only one thing that made it even better than it already was and that was the addition of another son, Caleb. We already had one busy guy by the name of Daniel, but adding Caleb to the mix made things even more interesting. The two boys were full of energy and were encouraged to enjoy living in their home just as much as we did.

Marcell and I always made it comfortable for them to play and have fun throughout the entire house. The carpet appeared to be very durable, but the vinyl flooring in the kitchen area took a beating from years of tough playing and constant walking. The boys liked to race their toy cars up and down the kitchen floor and roller skate too.

I know the vinyl floor was not made for this kind of punishment, but my husband and I wanted the boys to enjoy our home and have fond memories of living there. As you can probably imagine the kitchen floor received lots of dings and tears from the continual abuse by two active boys. Eventually the kitchen flooring needed to be replaced again.

As the boys grew older, their days of running, jumping, and playing on the kitchen floor ceased. They were finally becoming teenagers and I knew it was time to change the flooring again. I decided to price tile flooring just as a way to compare the cost of vinyl, but tile flooring was a little bit more expensive than regular vinyl. My mind was perplexed because I liked the look and durability of tile, but I knew vinyl was less expensive. Consequently, I let price dictate the purchase and I chose another vinyl floor rather than choosing a tile floor.

Almost immediately, I was unhappy with my purchase. The flooring I picked was very pretty, but the workmanship was not as nice. The gentleman I hired recommended that I leave the old flooring down and lay the new vinyl on top of the old to provide a cushion. That turned out to be a big mistake. I had two other vinyl floors underneath the current flooring and it never laid quite right.

Little did I know the man did not have the appropriate equipment to do the job properly. He never rolled out the glue bubbles in the flooring, so the floor had dimples and puckers all over it. Therefore, the floor never looked quite as good as it should have. The improper installation not only affected the look of the floor, but it also affected the long term durability of the product.

By this point, I knew I had made a big mistake in choosing another vinyl floor over a tile floor. Also hiring an unlicensed worker to lay the floor was another problem. My focus was on saving a few dollars rather than following my first instinct about a tile floor. Marcell always gave his opinion, but he allowed me to make the final decision about such matters. Generally speaking, we almost always agreed on changes to be made on the house.

Marcell's bottom line mostly aligned with price, while my decisions were more aligned with aesthetics. Somehow we always seemed to come to the same conclusion, although our approach was a little bit different.

As you might expect, the kitchen floor needed replacing a lot sooner than anticipated. I couldn't blame the need for a new floor on anyone but myself. That's why it took me about two years to finally broach the subject of changing the kitchen flooring again from vinyl to tile with Marcell.

This particular flooring did not last as long as it should have because of poor quality workmanship. I couldn't blame him for any part of the decision because I had taken the lead on this one. I fully accepted the fact that this floor was totally my responsibility and I was greatly dissatisfied with the outcome. When I had the opportunity to choose tile, I went the cheaper route and now I was unhappy.

I know this floor had not been down long, but it looked so bad I knew something had to be done soon. I realize my first initial thought about tile was the right one, and I should have followed my mind in the first place. I would have been right in- step with what was happening in new home construction for kitchens and bathrooms.

I truly believed that having the floor tiled was the right way to go this time and we would not have to change it again, ever! As I pondered over the idea, I thought this change to tile would be an easy sell. Of course, in my mind it was a great idea, but I knew Marcell wasn't going to be as easily persuaded because of the cost factor.

When I finally approached Marcell about changing the floors again, and told him I wanted tile on the floors instead of vinyl, I was met with unbridled opposition. The first thing Marcell questioned was the price. I couldn't argue with him about that because tile flooring was going to be more expensive than another vinyl floor.

The next argument was that there was potential danger in having tile in the kitchen and laundry room. He thought tile would be more slippery, increasing the possibility of falls. I told him that we could purchase tile that had a non-slip surface, which would eliminate that problem.

The possibility of the tile cracking was another concern. He had heard that tile was prone to crack if objects were dropped on it. I explained to him that cracks could be easily repaired and tile would end up being more cost effective in the long run.

I thought I had all the answers to each of his objections to laying tile, but somehow the only thing he could not get past was the price. Even though I thought I had pretty persuasive arguments in favor of tile, his bottom line came down to price. I couldn't believe he didn't see my view on this matter.

I thought to myself, "What is wrong with him? Can't he see how much better tile is going to be in the long term than vinyl? Doesn't he know this would be a real structural investment in our home?" Also, I thought the fact that we wouldn't have to do the floors again for a long time would have been a final incentive to seal the deal. It appeared as though my reasoning did not alter his opinion. He didn't seem to agree that the end product justified the price.

He could visibly see the floor needed changing just like I could. His remedy to the situation, however, was to surprise me with flooring that looked like tile, but was actually vinyl. He had the work done while I was out of town for a week. I know he thought I would be pleased because at first glance the floor looked like a tile floor, until you looked closer.

The truth is that I wasn't ever satisfied because I knew it wasn't really tile, but something made to resemble tile. It never passed the smell test for me. However, the one thing I could say about the vinyl flooring he had installed was that it was very nicely laid and it appeared to be of good quality.

I am sure in his mind he thought this would appease my desire for tile and address his issue with the price. I am also sure he thought this would keep me from being so dissatisfied with the decision to purchase more vinyl. I think under other conditions this would have been a good compromise for both of us, but it only made me more determined to get tile.

This issue became a little bone of contention as far as I was concerned. I felt he was merely looking at the price while I was looking at long-term value and benefits to the home. I know these things were important to him, but not as important as they were to me. I do give him props for the effort, but having said all of that, it did not change my mind. I wanted tile flooring in the kitchen and laundry room and I wasn't going to be satisfied with less. The campaign was on to make him change his mind.

Although the floors in the kitchen and laundry room looked good, I had made up my mind that I didn't like them and I felt unhappy because I wasn't getting my way. I made it known to Marcell, and anyone else who would listen, that I was campaigning for "real" tile floors in the kitchen and laundry room. I figured I would make the best out of the whole unpleasant situation until I could get the money to change it.

I wasn't sure how long this process would take, but I was willing to make some sacrifices in order to save up enough money for the required work. I knew what I wanted this time, and I wasn't going to be deterred from my goal. I think the more I talked about it, the less Marcell listened, which only made me angrier. I know it sounds illogical, but what can I say?

I think it goes without saying that both of us loved the house, but the list of work priorities revealed a sharp divide when it came to our approach to necessity. I wanted to close in the laundry room and make it a totally separate area from the garage because it wasn't climate controlled like the rest of the house. I also wanted to add an additional bathroom somewhere other than in the hallway near the sleeping areas. The final thing I wanted to do was to tile the kitchen and laundry room floors.

Although I had been talking about these things for a while, Marcell did not think they were as urgent as I did. However, somewhere in the back of my mind I knew they would happen. I didn't know how or when it would happen, but I knew it would happen if I just kept the faith.

I would periodically remind Marcell, "I still want tile on my kitchen and laundry room floors. I am planning to save enough money to get the work done as soon as possible."

His response was, "If that's what you want to do, then you do it, but I'm not going to put any money toward having it done. I already had the floor done and it looks good. I even went to the trouble to find some vinyl that looks exactly like tile and you still aren't satisfied."

"It's not that the floor doesn't look good, but I know in a few years we will have to have the floors replaced again. I don't want to do it later; I would rather do it now while we can really enjoy them."

His response remained firm that he would not get tile on the kitchen and laundry room floors. At this point I realized there was no need to talk to him any more about the issue because his mind was made up. Therefore, the best thing to do was to pray and leave it alone and make my own arrangements to get the flooring I desperately wanted.

Time has a way of moving on, and a situation that seemed so imperative at one point has a way of becoming less important at a different juncture in time. Other work needed to be done in the house and I didn't want to remain stuck on one improvement when there were other things we could do. Even though I never forgot my desire to have the kitchen and laundry room floors tiled, Marcell and I agreed to disagree.

We both decided it was time to give our hall bathroom a much needed face lift. I wanted to keep the same tub, but re-tile the walls inside the tub. He wanted to tear down the walls, remove the existing tub and replace, it with a one-piece tub and wall system. We both agreed the floor needed to be re-tiled and the wallpaper needed changing, but I thought replacing the existing tub with a one-piece system would be a big mistake. I didn't have any real proof concerning my objections, but I had that "woman's intuition" thing going on that I just couldn't shake.

Since he was the one paying the workers, Marcell decided to have the tub removed anyway against my better judgment and had it replaced with the one-piece tub system. Based on a recommendation from a friend, he hired a couple of guys from the local technical school to do the work. As the old saying goes, "When you don't listen to your wife, you get what you pay for."

I couldn't gloat too much because I had made several mistakes selecting workers myself in the past. I tried to talk him out of changing the tub, but his mind was made up that this would be a better look for the bathroom and an easier cleanup over the tile. Needless to say he was wrong on all counts. The one-piece tub system was awful!

When the work was finally done, I didn't like it at all, and neither did our sons. This time, it wasn't just because I had asked him not to do it. The tub was much harder to clean and was not properly lined up with the drain, so we couldn't keep the water from seeping out. The space inside the tub was smaller, and there was no real insulation between the tub and walls which resulted in less privacy when using the facilities. Not only did he have an unhappy wife, but he also had two unhappy sons as well.

The idea of having a nonslip surface in the tub sounded great, but it was much harder to keep clean. The interior space inside the tub turned out to be much smaller than our old tub. The boys weren't very happy and I wasn't very happy either. I didn't want to say, "I told you so," but I did tell him so.

I think the constant complaining got to him, so he decided to take the one-piece tub system down and re-tile the walls and put in a Jacuzzi instead. Hallelujah! That made everybody happy, including Marcell. This time he got a professional company to come in and do the work, and the result was great. We not only had the Jacuzzi put in to replace the tub, but we had the wall around the tub re-tiled with proper insulation, and the floor re-tiled as well.

The final thing we had done to the bathroom was to have the walls re-wallpapered. The old wallpaper had been on the walls since we moved into the house many years ago. It really needed some serious updating. We had the old wallpaper replaced with some new and modern wallpaper. The bathroom looked beautiful! Everything was coming together very nicely, and I felt good about what we had accomplished so far.

Everything was moving along very nicely and I was relatively happy with all the things we agreed to do in our home. However, I have heard it said that, "Women never forget when their mind is made up about a thing." I guess I can attest to this fact because, in the back of my mind, I kept thinking about my kitchen and laundry room floors. I stopped talking about it out loud because I didn't want to be considered a nag. I am sure Marcell thought I had forgotten about it because I stopped saying anything to him. I decided to pray more, and talk less, which is probably what God wanted me to do anyway.

Although my secret desire was to still have the kitchen and laundry room floors tiled, I stopped making a big issue out of it. It's funny how you finally figure out, "You are not in charge anyway, and as soon as you decide to let things go and let God handle it, that's when things start to happen. I don't think we ever fully understand how God can use such seemingly unimportant events in our lives to teach us deeply spiritual lessons, but that is what I think He does…as long as we remain open and willing to learn them.

It took me a minute to recognize that I had a lot of other positive things going on around me that needed my attention just as much as home improvements. I was always actively involved with the things that were going on with my children, and I was also interested in community work as well. Consequently, as I began to immerse myself in these things, I found I did not have time to complain about something as trivial as a floor. Furthermore, time was moving forward and it appeared that my children were growing up quickly and they needed my thoughts and prayers even more.

Before I knew it, our oldest son Daniel was graduating from high school and was ready to go off to college. Two years later he got married and moved to a different city. Two years after that our youngest son Caleb graduated from high school and he went off to college. By the grace of God my family was doing well. Even with the added expenses of college and other life events confronting us, Marcell and I were able to meet all our monthly obligations without a problem.

I recognized I was more than blessed with the life I was given and it was time for me to give back. I think whenever you do something to help others you do something to help yourself. God always has a plan and if we are patient, He has a way of working things out in our favor - even when we aren't aware of how He is doing it.

Marcell and I had so many wonderful things to be thankful for, I didn't have time to waste complaining about the few things I thought I deserved but didn't get. We had already had one bathroom updated a few years earlier, now it was time to make some improvements in the master bathroom. This time we both came to an understanding about what changes we wanted to make. We decided to re-tile the entire shower area. We knew the shower door would need replacing and we both agreed on a door that was just perfect. I was very much in favor of doing the work, but this time I didn't want to become too entrenched in the process.

By this time, I had found other outside interests that kept me busy. I, by no means, abrogated my duties and responsibilities for the changes we were working on in the house. I certainly wanted my opinions taken into consideration as we picked patterns and colors for the walls and floors in the master bath, but I didn't want to become too dogmatic with my opinions. Marcell and I have always had pretty similar taste when it comes to things we like, so when we went to the store, we found just the right tile for the walls and floor.

Once everything was in place, we agreed that while I was gone to visit my parents during the summer he would have the work done just as we had agreed. When I returned home everything looked beautiful! It certainly gave the place a new look and a new appeal. However, one more thing was done that was an unexpected and pleasant surprise: he had new tile floors put in the kitchen and laundry room. I couldn't believe it! After all this time he actually had the work done and it looked absolutely marvelous!

In my wildest dreams I never had a clue Marcell was going to have the kitchen and laundry room floors tiled. It had been many years since we had even talked about it. I figured he was just ignoring me because of my constant complaining in the past. I never saw it coming and I don't think I could have hoped for better than what I got. It had been quite a few years since I had mentioned the kitchen and laundry room floors to him. This work was so unexpected, but so much appreciated. It brought tears to my eyes and gratitude to my heart for having such a man as Marcell.

He had selected a white tile that perfectly matched the wallpaper and the counter tops in the kitchen. This gave the area a whole new look and a much needed face lift. It took me aback at what good taste he had. I couldn't have been happier if I had picked it myself. The most amazing thing is that I had completely let the whole matter drop, but God had not forgotten about my secret prayer. To others, this might be a trivial matter not worthy of an honorable mention, but God has shown me He is concerned about every little detail of our lives if we give it to him.

All of a sudden, the light came on for me and now I understood what this whole lesson was all about. It had nothing to do with tile or floors at all. I felt so enlightened and could clearly see the principal of what I had missed so many years ago because I was "sweating the small stuff."

I think sometimes we become too obsessed with our own wants and desires and we can't see the bigger picture right in front of us. Sometimes we forget there is a bigger plan for our lives in play. Furthermore, we feel our prayers are not being heard and we go around feeling disappointed because things aren't happening fast enough for us. as I reflect back, it became much clearer to me that God never works on our time schedule. I came to the realization that He has His own time schedule for our lives.

The one thing I really learned was how to wait on God. I know I was impatient and I needed to learn how to wait. Things don't always happen right when we expect them to, but they happen when they are supposed to happen. I also had to learn to care about the feelings of someone else other than myself – particularly, the feelings of my husband.

I thought this whole episode about tile was to teach me to wait on God because He would fulfill the desires of my heart. I soon found out that God had a greater purpose and a bigger lesson for me to learn. He wanted to teach me gratitude and trust. Gratitude for the things He has given me and to trust in Him enough to know He knows what is best for me.

I think I am like every other typical person who quotes the scripture in Matthew 7:7, which says, "Ask and it shall be given, seek and ye shall find, knock and the door shall be opened unto you." We take it to mean, "God will give me everything I want when I want it."

I know God hears us and tolerates us in our ignorance and selfishness. Many times He gives us the desires of our heart even though we don't deserve it. Most of the time, we only care about what we want and not how it impacts others. I think He was giving me time to grow and mature into the woman He ultimately wanted me to become, but I had to go through the lessons and recognize that each lesson is designed to help me grow and lead me to a greater destiny for my life.

It feels great when we get the things we want or think we want, but how do we behave when the things we want don't come right away? I think this is the real test of our character and our love meter. I never considered myself as having a microwave personality, but that is exactly the example I was exhibiting: "I want what I want and I want it right now." God knew there were other factors that needed to be taken into consideration besides my ever-changing whims.

I really thought I had the patience thing down pat, but what I found I was doing very well was marking time until I could get what I wanted. Patience is a great virtue to have, but it takes a lot of practice and a lot of waiting to ultimately build genuine patience. I don't know if you ever get to the point that you have all the patience you will ever need, but I have learned that each level helps you build yourself more and more as you go through each situation.

I am glad I finally got the floors I wanted in the house, but I am more excited that I learned something about myself, my husband, and my God at the same time. Life is what you make it, so don't waste a minute feeling sorry for yourself. Learn to be thankful for what you have. Complain less and praise more.

Debra A. K. Thompson

PART VI

The Winning Campaigns

Marcell and I always thought of ourselves as community-minded people who were always interested in things going on around us. We maintained memberships in the NAACP, SCLC, NBCDI, and BIG, as well as several other community organizations that had local chapters. However, two of these organizations would lead us down a path that would change the trajectory of our lives and propel us onto a different course even greater than we could have ever foreseen.

The path I thought we would take – work hard, raise our children and then retire – is not the straight path we actually followed. I learned that things are not always the way they seem. There may be detours in the road and new lessons to grasp.

The first scenario involved a local grassroots organization called Progressive Alliance Community Equity Resources and Strategies (PACERS,) subsequently changed to Movement for Change (MFC,) and their effort to have a street named after Dr. Martin Luther King, Jr. The second scenario involved a locally owned Black television station called WBOP-TV (which was later changed to WBQP-TV,) and their battle to remain on the local cable line-up.

One evening in 1997 while listening to the Community Awareness Show on WRNE Radio, Marcell and I heard a story about a local group who were involved in an effort to have a street named after Dr. Martin Luther King, Jr. The group leading this venture was Movement for Change. Our friend, Mr. Antonio Caldwell, was the person leading the group and spearheading the charge. Apparently this group had been trying to get a street named after Dr. King for quite a while with no success.

On its face, it sounded like something that should have been an easy request to address. Based on the tone of the conversation, there were numerous unexpected hurdles that they had to overcome if their request was to be granted by the Pensacola City Council. The group, according to the discussion, seemed to face strong opposition from the Council despite their efforts to comply with their requests. As Marcell and I continued to listen, Mr. Caldwell concluded by his remarks that discrimination might be playing a role in the difficulties they were having. I don't think Marcell or I had enough information at that time to make a decision whether or not discrimination by the Council was, in fact, occurring, but Movement for Change and Mr. Caldwell believed it to be the case.

As we continued to listen to the report, I just couldn't imagine what was so hard about their request. I surmised this should have been an easy problem to fix, but apparently the name change process might not have been as simple as I thought. In my mind, I just didn't want to believe the reaction of the group was justified. However, it appeared that this subject was rapidly becoming a sore spot with MFC because it was taking longer than the organizers had anticipated.

As we continued to listen I told my husband, "There must be something Movement for Change is doing wrong. They're probably not following the correct procedures in order to get the street renamed."

Marcell replied, "You are probably right. How hard can it be to get a street renamed? I wouldn't think this would be a major undertaking." Marcell and I seem to share the same opinion on the matter and we promptly dismissed the whole report from our minds and continued with our evening ritual.

I think Marcell and I realized this was an important topic, but we didn't think about it too seriously until one evening, as destiny would have it, we happened to see Mr. Antonio Caldwell on television. He was getting ready to speak at a Pensacola City

Council meeting. Normally, we never watched the City Council meetings, but on this particular evening, we were channel surfing when we saw him. His topic was, "Renaming a street after Dr. King." He was appearing before the Council in a section of the meeting called, Open Forum.

From what I observed, Mr. Caldwell was trying to make his case for naming a street after Dr. King. As we listened, he explained that he and the group, MFC, had been before the Council on numerous occasions concerning this matter, but he was always asked to go back and choose another street instead of the one they had chosen. He went on to state that he brought a new list of streets for consideration for a name change to Dr. Martin Luther King, Jr. Drive and he hoped one of them would be approved by the Council members.

In my mind as I sat and listened, I felt so disappointed because it did not seem feasible that a request which sounded so simple on its face was creating such a stir. Again, I thought to myself, "MFC must be doing something wrong because surely it can't be that tough to change a street name."

I am not so naive that I don't recognize that prejudice is still alive and well, but I couldn't imagine why anyone would not want to name a street after Dr. Martin Luther King, Jr. I didn't want to believe it was the old fallback position of "prejudice." Therefore, I could only conclude this group was doing something incorrectly. I just didn't want to think people who were elected to a public office would not sympathize and do everything they could to make this request possible. Yet, as we continued to watch, the Council seemed to listen very intently to his words. They were very polite, but it was very obvious to me by their expressions and demeanor that they had no intention of addressing his request.

I had never watched a council meeting before that evening, and I am not sure what I expected to see, but what they did certainly wasn't it. I heard Mr. Caldwell explain, "We have done everything you asked. We have come up with several different alternatives to your prior objections, yet you will not address our request."

It was very eerie to watch, but the stone faced group remained silent, allowing his time to elapse. Then they simply called the next speaker. I was appalled at what I considered rude treatment of a citizen. After watching this, I told Marcell, "We should attend one of the MFC meetings to find out more about them and their request." I wanted to understand the Council's real objections and see what, if anything, could be done to resolve this issue. I didn't know if we could do anything to help, but I felt a strong desire to find out more.

I felt so dismayed over what we had just witnessed on television I couldn't wait until we could get to an MFC meeting. We made a few phone calls and found out the Movement for Change group held their meetings on Thursday evenings at one of the local churches. Marcell and I planned to attend the very next meeting.

When that day arrived, I was very surprised to see so many people at the meeting. Apparently a lot of other people in the community saw Mr. Caldwell's appearance before the City Council and had some of the same concerns we had. The place was packed full with mostly African-Americans, but there were Whites, Hispanics, young and old in attendance. It appeared that most of the people did not really understand the Council's objection to naming a street after Dr. Martin Luther King either.

I probably asked the same question every first time attendee wanted to ask, "What are you doing, or not doing, to comply with the requirements of City Council? I don't understand why getting a street named after Dr. King should be such a long and difficult task. What needs to be done to make them say 'yes?'"

After listening to all the comments and questions, Mr. Caldwell proceeded to explain the process they followed to make their request for naming a street after Dr. King. "The process began over a year ago. I and several other members of the organization went down to City Hall to ascertain the proper procedures for requesting a street name change. We were given several forms to fill out. Once those forms were completed, the next step was to forward them to the Planning Department for research and assessment. When the Planning Department completed its assessment, the request would then be given to City Council for final approval. However, as of this date, our request has not been approved. We have only been given more hurdles to overcome. I am personally aware of several streets in the City that have been renamed in the recent past, and it did not take a long time to get it done. That's why I am so astonished at the push back from City Council about this request."

He then recounted the names of several streets they suggested to the Council as potential compromise locations to the originally requested street. "The first street we requested was Palafox Street. We were told that Palafox Street was part of the county and the State of Florida jurisdiction and probably would not be approved. The next choice was Davis Street and it was turned down for similar reasons. Another suggestion was 'A' Street. This street was a smaller street and was not a part of a major highway. It, too, was turned down. We made numerous efforts to come up with a street that the Council would approve, but none of our suggestions were accepted. So our final request was Alcaniz Street, and this time we weren't willing to take 'no' for an answer."

After hearing all of the steps they had taken to find a suitable street to rename after Dr. King, the general consensus in the room was that the Council was probably being unfair. It sounded like MFC was willing to compromise, but nothing they suggested was acceptable.

My attitude was: "If the Council did not like any of the names being proposed by the group, what was their alternative?" In my opinion, they didn't seem to have an alternative, just excuses. Their excuses sounded very weak, thin, lame, and unbelievable to me. Consequently, many of the community members like me started thinking discrimination might be playing a role in the continuous denial by the Council. I am not saying it was true, but the perception was undeniable given the information we received during the meeting.

After listening to everything Mr. Caldwell had to say, Marcell and I still felt baffled at the Council's objections to this request. It felt like a reasonable petition to make, given that MFC appeared to be willing to compromise. By this time, many cities around the country had streets named after Dr. King, and it wasn't an unreasonable expectation that our City could do the same. That's why I think we developed a real interest in this issue. As a result, we decided to become more actively involved with MFC to help in this effort. Our decision to work with this group would prove to be a good choice – one that would affect our lives forever.

Once Marcell and I became actively involved with MFC, we worked tirelessly, along with the other members of the organization, to get a street named after Dr. King. We started attending City Council meetings, County Commission meetings, and School Board meetings to learn more about the inner-workings of our local government. We participated in planning sessions and strategy sessions to bring more awareness to our plight.

However, sometimes God has a way of maneuvering other important issues into your purview that seem to have no relationship to your original goal. While we were so focused on the issue of getting a street named after Dr. King, a second destiny-altering experience occurred. It involved our close friends, Charles and Vivian Bridgeton, who owned a low-power television station, WBOP-TV. We were not aware of the struggle they were encountering trying to maintain their station on the local cable line-up.

Marcell and I became acquainted with the Bridgeton's back in the early 80's. Marcell and Vivian worked at the same command at the Naval Air Station. Charles and I worked at the Naval Air Station as well, but in different commands. Once we all became friends, I found Charles to be a hard-working man with big dreams just like Marcell. Vivian and I were very similar in attitude because we were always in support of our husbands, regardless of their ventures. They both had that entrepreneurial spirit, so it was an easy association to make.

As friends, Marcell found he and Charles had many interests in common. They were both enamored with still photography and the new technology of video cameras. Charles and Vivian already had a small business called Prestige Video that they operated with another couple by the name of Joe and Wanda Vester. Joe worked at the local water plant and Wanda was a school teacher. They handled the photography end of the business while Charles and Vivian worked in the video end of the business. Since Marcell really enjoyed photography and video they asked us to join them in Prestige Video. Together we formed the "Wedding Connection" that would provide wedding video and photography services for many couples in the area for several years.

After approximately six to eight years of operating Prestige Video, Charles obtained information about purchasing a low-power television station. He thought this was a great chance for our team to expand our focus from strictly video and photography to television production. We all thought it was a good opportunity, but the only couple who came up with funds to purchase the station was Charles and Vivian.

Truthfully speaking, I think they were the only ones who saw the long-term vision of what a low-power television station could mean to the Pensacola community. Eventually the members of our team decided we would dissolve our partnership and pursue our own business ventures. Charles and Vivian decided they wanted to keep the name Prestige Video for the production end of their business, but named the television station "WBOP-TV." Joe and Wanda decided they wanted to stay in the photography end of the business while Marcell and I continued to work in video. Since Charles and Vivian were moving more into the television side of production with Prestige Video, Marcell and I decided to start our own video company and we named it "A Artistic Video."

Although we kept ourselves busy developing and growing A Artistic Video, that didn't preclude us from getting involved with WBOP and assisting where we could. The programming on the new television station primarily targeted African-American viewers, but they had shows that a wide cross-section of the community could enjoy. What made it even better is the fact that Charles and Vivian were eventually able to secure cable access for the station through the local cable company, known as Cox Cable.

During that period of time, there was only one other network that offered African-American programming to our area through the cable company besides WBOP and that was Black Entertainment Television (BET.) I don't think WBOP-TV was ever designed to be a replacement for BET, but it was definitely a viable alternative because of its local flavor.

The difference between BET and WBOP was that WBOP was locally owned and operated. They also offered local talent and local businesses a chance to shine. I know I wasn't the only one who felt pride in having a station like WBOP-TV located in our community. I think most people recognized the benefits, along with the prestige, in having them there. Most of all I was happy I could call Charles and Vivian my friends. I considered it a privilege to have the option to work with them as I began to expand my horizons.

After a few years of operation, WBOP-TV soon changed its name to WBQP-TV. Everything appeared to be going well for Charles and Vivian. The station proved to be a wonderful investment for them. Additionally, it gave voice to the issues in the local Black Community, who were often ignored by the mainstream media.

It also gave local people like me a chance to produce and create original shows. One of the programs I helped to develop, produce, and host on the station was "The Gospel Express," which was a spin-off from the "Gospel Express Magazine," which I published. I also hosted another live call-in show entitled, "In Time," which was an informational program. I created and hosted a show with my friend Jennifer Long called, "It's Your Business," another live call-in show that answered questions about business and business-related practices. All of these activities were in addition to my responsibilities as a wife and mother. As you can see, I was a very busy girl. I've always led a full life and this period of time was no exception.

One evening while attending one of our regular MFC meetings, someone brought up the fact that WBQP-TV had been removed from the local cable line-up. I was quite surprised at the news because I had not heard anything like this from Charles or Vivian. I knew they had worked long and hard to obtain cable access, that's why I was taken aback at this news. I just assumed everything was going well because I had not heard anything to the contrary.

I periodically watched a number of shows on the station, but was unaware of the recent change. The speaker expressed concern because WBQP was not just the only African-American owned television station in Pensacola, but it was the only one in the State of Florida. This fact was unique all by itself. As he continued to speak, he said, "The station is still on the air, but can only be accessed if the viewers have an outside antenna."

Upon hearing this information, I felt very concerned. I did not want to lose this community treasure from the cable line-up either. Marcell and I did not have an outside antenna. Therefore, it would be difficult for us to watch the station as well.

As the speaker continued to relay his information, he said he saw this as an attempt by the cable company to force WBQP-TV out of business. I didn't know if his assessment was true, but he emphasized that they would not be able to obtain advertising dollars with such limited viewership. He further stated that the Bridgeton's had worked long and hard to finally get their station on the cable system. To now have it removed suddenly without explanation seemed to be unimaginable, unthinkable, and unfathomable.

I know I wasn't the only one stunned by the information being presented. Several people asked questions trying to ascertain the facts surrounding the removal. I had questions of my own because I thought this matter, if true, would some immediate community intervention. One of the most important questions being asked was, "What happened? What precipitated this sudden removal?"

The speaker indicated he wasn't privy to any of the underlying politics of this decision, but he knew money played a significant role in the decision. He thought the Bridgetons could use our support. That's why he came to MFC, because he thought we might be able to intervene and help resolve the problem before things got out of hand.

Many in the Black community embraced WBQP and saw it as a source of pride for the entire Pensacola community. The Bridgetons had achieved something that most people, Black or White, could not accomplish: Operation of a television station. I certainly didn't want to see this treasure lost without knowing what happened.

Even hearing what the speaker had to say, I still didn't quite understand what had precipitated this action. I thought the concern of the speaker warranted further investigation just to assure the community that something was being done. Most of the people in the room had some familiarity with the Bridgetons and WBQP-TV, but had no real insight about this matter at all. After the speaker completed his presentation and answered all the questions he could from the audience, Mr. Caldwell took the podium.

Mr. Caldwell had a very concerned look on his face. He thanked the speaker for bringing this important information about WBQP to our attention. He totally agreed with the speaker's assessment and thought this was an issue worthy of further investigation. However, he reminded everyone that our primary focus was getting a street named after Dr. King. He thought MFC could certainly play a role, in helping WBQP, but not necessarily take the lead.

"We don't have the human resources available to divide our focus and continue to achieve our goal." Mr. Caldwell cautioned. As I sat there listening, I completely understood his reasoning. But I knew, if true, something had to be done and I wanted to be a part of it. Therefore, I volunteered my services to aid in this query.

Although I had never been in charge of such an important community effort like this, I decided this was something I could support and take the lead. I wasn't doing it just because Charles and Vivian were my friends. It's just that I couldn't understand how a wonderful station like WBQP could be pulled from the cable line-up without warning. I knew there was probably more to the story than was being discussed at the meeting, but I needed to know more. Consequently, I thought I might be able to assist my friends if I had all the pertinent information surrounding their deletion from the cable programming. I felt pretty confident that others would support me in this endeavor if they knew all the facts too. My goal, if possible, was to get WBQP back on the cable line-up. I was determined to make that happen, but only if I could rally support from the community.

The first thing I needed to know was what happened to precipitate their removal. The only way to answer this question was to speak with Charles Bridgeton directly. I thought it might be important to hear what he had to say before making any plans or drawing any conclusions. I wanted to make sure he needed and wanted our support. So when I called him, he was glad to know that I, along with the members of MFC, was interested in helping him with this endeavor. He didn't know if we could really do a lot to help him, but he was appreciative of any support we could give.

As he began to recount the facts to me, he reiterated that his station was a low-power station not a high-power station. This meant the signal only reached a small segment of the population with the assistance of an antenna of some kind. That's why cable access was so important. High-power stations, on the other hand, usually carry stronger signals and have a broader reach. By Federal Communication Commission (FCC) standards, cable systems must air programming from high-power stations, but have the discretion in working with low-power stations. The low-power station, unlike a high-power station, could be assessed a fee for using the cable system for airing their programming.

Since they were designated as a low-power station, the cable company did not have to automatically place them in their line-up. The cable company had the right to charge them virtually whatever amount they deemed appropriate to charge. Charles knew he was negotiating from a disadvantaged standpoint, but he needed the services the cable system had to offer if his station was to survive and thrive. Consequently, it took a lot of bargaining to finally secure an amount they could potentially afford to be on the cable line-up.

Although the price was higher than he anticipated, Charles thought having cable access was an important enough accomplishment to try. This was a good thing because it meant that a broader cross-section of the community could view their programming and they could solicit more advertising dollars to help meet their monthly expenses. Even though it was a struggle each month to make their payments, somehow they managed to stay afloat for quite a while. Initially the plan to secure more advertising dollars worked well, but once they got behind, it was a futile struggle to catch up.

As I queried Charles a little further, he admitted the advertising dollars they raised were never quite enough to meet their monthly obligations. He and Vivian continued to struggle on by supplementing the expenses with their own personal finances. Their goal was to provide quality shows for the community, even though it came at a great personal sacrifice.

To add insult to injury, Charles learned that there were a couple of other low-power stations in our community whose fees were different from that of WBQP. Upon learning this information, he requested a rate adjustment, but that was denied. Charles was reasonably sure no other low-power station in the area was being charged the high rate applied to them. He did not expect free services, but he did expect a fair and equitable deal.

In the meantime, the cable company executives refused to negotiate any further with them because they were behind on their payments. Subsequently, WBQP was finally removed from the cable line-up. As a last resort, Charles hoped MFC could help them gain more public support and shed light on their dilemma. Charles further believed this move might pressure the Cable representatives into negotiating a more fair and equitable package for WBQP-TV. He thought the cable company was being arbitrary and capricious with their pricing. This made it almost impossible for them to get back on the air without help.

After my conversation with Charles and hearing all the facts, I proceeded to call a meeting with community members who were interested in finding out more about WBQP's abrupt removal from the cable line-up. I wanted to lay out all of the facts and solicit support at the same time. I felt impassioned and energized to move forward since I understood the problem better.

Marcell and a few of my close friends joined the bandwagon with me in support of the station. After laying out all the facts of the situation, I was very pleased that so many in the community agreed with my view of the circumstances and showed their support by agreeing to work with me. Marcell was one of my most ardent supporters, and he made sure I was able to attend any meetings necessary to strategize our plans.

Before we got to the community meeting, my friend Jennifer and I created several sample letters to send to the cable company in support of reinstating WBQP-TV to their program line-up. We knew that everyone wouldn't want to write a letter, but maybe offering a pre-written letter might encourage more people to participate. We figured that some people would prefer to write their own letter, however, some people might need a little more help. If the form letters we wrote were approved, then all people had to do was sign, date, and mail the letter to the cable company.

The letters simply read in-part: "We are displeased at the decision to remove WBQP-TV from the regular line-up of stations airing through the Cox Cable System and we request that WBQP-TV be immediately reinstated and a more equitable fee be negotiated. If this request is not accepted, we the community members will discontinue our cable service in protest of the decision."

Once we brought the letters to the meeting for people to read, they were a big hit. Most of the attendees of the meeting signed more than one letter. Some people even took letters with them to get others to sign who did not attend the meeting. Those who signed a letter that night also made a monetary donation to help with postage for mailing the letters that were collected. We were off to a great start. We were fueled by the knowledge that our cause was just and filled with the optimism to believe we could win if we stayed the course.

The second thing we did was to organize a telephone campaign to flood the cable company with calls requesting that WBQP TV be reinstated. The final thing we decided to do was to write letters to the Federal Communications Commission (FCC) to ask for assistance in this matter. We did not know if any of our strategies would work, but we knew for sure it would bring more visibility to the problem. We knew this was not going to be an over-night fix. It would take tenacity, hard work, and dedication to accomplish the desired results: Reinstatement of WBQP on the cable line-up.

We met every week for several months for the purpose of obtaining more signed letters to send to the cable company. Additionally, we asked everyone to call customer service each day and leave messages of displeasure over the removal of WBQP-TV from the cable line-up. Based on the positive feedback we received each week, it was apparent a vast number of community members were just as distraught over the news about WBQP and wanted to help.

However, as you well know, in every campaign there are always detractors and devil's advocates who do not agree with your methods and are there merely to distract you from your goal. This effort was no exception. We had some who thought the Bridgetons should pay whatever amount the cable company charged, or not utilize their services. Others thought this effort was worthwhile, but felt some people would not write letters and make calls as requested. Still others thought people would not follow through on discontinuing their cable services if our demands were not met. I am sure I was being a little more optimistic than most, but I had faith people would follow through on their commitment if they truly believed in the cause.

Marcell and I, along with many others in our group, discontinued our cable services. We wanted the cable company to know we were serious about our demands. We wanted to apply all the economic pressure we could invoke to make our position clear. We had no unrealistic expectations that this effort would be resolved overnight, but we knew if we could keep up the pressure, they might be willing to return to the negotiating table and deal more compassionately with WBQP. As the letter writing campaign continued, several hundred letters were signed and sent to the local cable company each week. Hundreds of calls were made to Cox and to the FCC. It took several months before we finally received some positive news…WBQP-TV had been reinstated!

I know there were some things going on behind the scenes that we in the community did not have privy to know, but I feel reasonably sure public pressure and scrutiny hastened negotiations. I can't confirm that my efforts, along with the efforts of the community, were the only reason the cable company relented, but I know that our actions contributed to the end result.

Regardless of how much impact our group had, I felt very proud to play some small role in helping my friends get back on the cable line-up. I think this gave me hope that other issues like naming a street after Dr. King could be just as easily addressed with similar results.

I never thought of myself as a very political person, and if you had asked me prior to the WBQP episode, I would have told you, "I don't do politics." Of course, my husband and I were avid voters and we always kept up with the news and the local happenings, but before that time, we never took the front position. We were always behind the scenes as supporters.

We both loved working in the community and we were always looking for ways to help make our community a better place to live. However, I think the WBQP-TV campaign sparked something deep within me that helped me to realize change is possible only if people like me are willing to help make it happen.

As Marcell and I continued to attend Movement for Change meetings, I started learning more and more about the function of City Council. I could also see for myself how unyielding the majority of the Council was in their objections to naming a street after Dr. King. It appeared that they could never get the issue approved to move forward for a vote. Each time the issue was brought forward, there were not enough votes to support the motion.

There was only one Black Council member serving at that time, Ms. Eunice G. Floyd, and she could never get a second when she raised the issue about Dr. King Street. Therefore, they had to keep raising the issue during the open forum portion of the meeting. I was so distraught over the fact that these citizens were petitioning their Council members for what seemed to be a simple request, but their requests seem to fall on deaf ears. I wasn't sure how a City Council person should respond to a citizen request, but I knew the way it was being handled wasn't right either.

Each time we went to an MFC meeting or a City Council meeting, I came home feeling frustrated. I didn't know what more we could do, but I knew more had to be done if Pensacola was ever going to have a street named after Dr. King. I kept telling Marcell, "Somebody should do something."

"Who is 'somebody,' Taffnee? You keep complaining, so why don't you do something about it. You are somebody, so why can't you do something besides complain."

I immediately went into defense mode, "What can I do? I am only one person."

"Why don't you run for City Council?"

"Who, me? I am not qualified to do anything like that, Marcell. Besides, nobody would ever vote for me. I'm not a politician. I'm just a plain-old everyday citizen who has no experience in politics."

"Taffnee, you may not be a politician, but maybe that's what is needed in this situation. Complaining to me won't change a thing."

Up until that point, I had never considered running for any kind of public office. I considered myself as just an average citizen who exercised my right to vote, took care of my family, and worked in my community. The idea almost seemed too implausible to imagine, but it was an intriguing thought.
I didn't believe people like me could get into politics and actually win an election. But here I was wondering if I could really do it.

As I pondered over his words, I thought to myself, "He is right. What good is complaining to him doing?"

It's just like Mahatma Gandhi said, "Be the change you want to see in the world." That's when I knew that, if I wanted change to happen, I must become the change agent I was seeking, not wait on someone else to do it.

I said to Marcell, "Maybe you're right. What do I need to do?" He suggested we speak with Mr. Caldwell to see what he thought about my running for City Council.

When we finally made that call to Mr. Caldwell, he seemed very enthusiastic and thought it was a great idea for me to run. He stated that he had been trying to encourage more people to run for public office, but it was hard to get people to commit. He then suggested we contact the Supervisor of Elections Office to get more information. If I was really serious, he said he would be willing to help. He then urged us to review everything carefully and let him know when we were ready to move forward.

After reviewing all the appropriate paperwork, Marcell thought we should examine each eligible seat carefully before making a choice. The Pensacola City Council at that time was made up of 10 Council members and a Ceremonial Mayor. There were seven single- member district seats and three at-large seats. There was a total of eight White males, one White female and one Black female who made up the council.

Three of the seats were considered minority/majority seats (Districts 5, 6 and 7). Only one of the minority/majority district seats was held by an African-American, and that was Ms. Eunice G. Floyd. There had been other African-Americans who had served on the council in prior years, but she was the only one currently serving.

The only district seat I was eligible to seek was District 1, but that seat was occupied by Mr. Terry Washburn, a long-time veteran Council member. Marcell thought this seat might be harder to win because I was an unknown opponent. Being the methodical strategist he has always been, Marcell thought I should run for an at-large seat on the Council. Marcell found out that there were three at-large seats: two of them were occupied by individuals who had been on the Council for many years, but the third person, Wayne Fitzmeyer, had recently been appointed to his at-large seat and might be the easiest person to challenge.

It appeared that Mr. Fitzmeyer had vacated his District 6 seat after serving only one year of a two-year term in that position. He was a White male who had been elected in a majority Black district. Many of the voters were unhappy with his decision to vacate the seat after they had elected him to the position. It not only left a vacant seat in the district, but it also left some disgruntled citizens who felt betrayed once he was appointed to the at-large Seat. Marcell thought this fact could work in my favor and be the key to my success.

Marcell also discovered that, although a few African-Americans had been appointed to serve on Council in an at-large capacity, none had ever won the position through the election process. Mr. Fitzmeyer had never run for an at-large seat either, but he had some voters who might be willing to vote for me because of his earlier decision to leave his District 6 Council Seat. It was a long-shot, but it seemed like the best alternative if I had any hope of winning.

The next step on my journey to City Council was to find out if there was any support for me in the community if I decided to run. The first place I started was with the members of our grassroots organization to see if they would be willing to back my campaign.

They asked me some hard questions: "Why are you running? What do you think you can do to help the community? Would you be willing to support naming a street after Dr. Martin Luther King, Jr.?" I must admit this whole process was all very new to me, but I knew I needed their support if I was going to win. This was a real campaign and I was expected to answer difficult questions just like any other contender. Although I felt a little shaky, I answered all their questions to the best of my ability. As a result, I received whole-hearted support from the organization.

Once I received their support, I knew I could move to the next step of qualifying for the office of Pensacola City Council.

There were two ways in which I could qualify to run for City Council: pay the qualification fee or qualify by petition. Marcell thought it would be better for me to qualify by petition because this gave me the opportunity to meet people and let them get to know me. Since I was a virtual unknown, people could ask me questions and become familiar with my name.

I am thankful I did not have to do this alone. Marcell, along with many members of MFC, were able to help me obtain the appropriate number of voter cards for me to qualify. Once I qualified, I had the arduous task of raising money for my campaign as well.

Marcell worked diligently as my campaign manager and helped me formulate a plan for potentially winning this City Council seat. It was very reassuring to have two of my closest friends, Jennifer Long and Lucinda Jacobs, in my corner to help me garner support. I don't think many people thought I could really win this seat, but they were willing to give me a chance.
Honestly, I don't know if I thought I could win either. but I had to give it the "good old college try."

Once the campaign was in full-swing, it was amazing to me that so many people got on the bandwagon in my support. I felt the enthusiasm and the support from so many people who did not know me personally, but were willing to hear what I had to say and give me a chance.

To my surprise, when the votes were all tallied, I was the winner! I couldn't believe it, but I had actually won a seat on the Pensacola City Council. It felt like a dream to me, but it was really true. A virtual unknown was able to convince a majority of the citizens to give me a chance to represent them as their City Council Member At-Large.

The other amazing thing that happened during this campaign season was that there were two other African-Americans elected at the same time I was elected: Reverend Amos Riley for District 6 and Ms. Betina Erickson for District 7. Along with myself and Ms. Eunice G. Floyd, this made a total of 4 Blacks now serving on the Pensacola City Council. How amazing was that?

God was the orchestrator of it all. To my knowledge, there had never been that many African-Americans serving on the Council before. I know I wasn't the only one who felt pride when we were all sworn-in, but I think it was an awe inspiring moment for the entire community.

I also think a renewed enthusiasm for the voting process prevailed over our community as this election cycle ended and a new era unfolded. Before this time, there had been so many defeats on so many levels that a blanket of weariness seemed to cover the landscape until this election gave promise to endless opportunity. People felt the stagnation and quagmire of despair, but an unexpected win had everyone feeling hopeful, ready to work, and ready to take on the next challenge.

The celebration was over and I knew it was time to get down to some real City Council business. I didn't know how long it would be before Mr. Caldwell and the members of MFC would be standing in front of the City Council requesting a street be named after Dr. Martin Luther King, Jr., but I knew they would be coming soon. I knew they were giving me along with the other new members of the Council, a chance to become acclimated to our new positions, but I also knew they were coming.

I also knew that the City Council operated under the "Sunshine Law," which meant I could not discuss any matter that might come before the Council for a vote with any other Council Member. All the business coming before the Council had to be discussed in the eye of the public. Consequently, I had no idea how any other Council member felt about Dr. King Street, or how they would vote if the matter was presented. I only knew how I felt and how I would vote.

I was aware that there was a segment of the community who were opposed to renaming Alcaniz Street after Dr. King. Their argument was that Alcaniz Street was a historic street and should not be touched. However, that claim had been used for almost every other street brought forward by MFC for consideration in the past.

To make matters worse, the previous Council had no other recommendations and offered no compromise to the group. That seemed to be the major problem for the proponents of naming a street after Dr. King. Apparently, no street being suggested met with the approval of the opposition. That created a stand-off so that nothing got done. At this point, a compromise seemed very unlikely if something did not change.

I would like to think that God in His infinite wisdom waited until there were enough new faces and perspectives on the Council to make something happen. As you can probably guess, we were able to place the topic of Dr. King Street on the Council agenda for discussion. When Mr. Caldwell came up to address the Council as he had done so many times before, I was able to give him an opportunity to fully present his case.

After he finished speaking, this time instead of being heard and summarily dismissed, to my surprise Councilman Harry Goldsmith made a motion to rename a portion of Alcaniz Street within the City limits to "Dr. Martin Luther King, Jr., Drive." I quickly seconded the motion. This meant the Council could thoroughly discuss the motion on the floor and could potentially bring it to a vote. This time we had enough Council members who voted in favor of the motion. Finally, after all this time, Pensacola had a street named after Dr. King!

I can't take total credit for this outcome, but who is to say God didn't have me in this pivotal role? "For such a time as this?" Esther 4:14. I know that God can use anyone in any situation He so chooses to fulfill His will. I am glad I became enlightened enough to understand what I needed to learn through this sojourn. Although, I had no idea when I volunteered to help with WBQP-TV so many years before that I would eventually end up on the Pensacola City Council. However, I know God knew all the time what was needed and helped me to prepare for the journey.

Looking back on it now, I can see how God was directing my path. He had me at the right place at the right time to be of service to the community. My election proved to be a significant event in my life and in the history of Pensacola. The work with the WBQP-TV project and my work with Movement for Change helped me to gain favor with many of the citizens who would not have ordinarily known me or voted for me. Moreover, I was in a position to help bridge the chasm between the City Council and the Black Community concerning renaming a street after Dr. Martin Luther King, Jr.

I know this entire period in Pensacola history is very important, and I am glad I could play some small role in it. I truly realize I am not where I am because of who I am, but I am where I am because of who God is in me.

I am so glad I had the opportunity to serve my community and play some small role in shaping key events surrounding my life. Sometimes you can really feel you have nothing to offer, but every situation happens so you can learn something and share something. The learning and sharing part may not always be clear, but if you remain faithful and diligent, God has a way of revealing it all to you. Don't ever think your role is insignificant because every aspect, no matter how big or small, is needed. I have found that even a screw has an important job to do.

People ask me all the time if I will ever return to the political arena. My answer is always, "No." However, I must temper my answer with, "Whatever God has for me to do, I'm willing to do it."

I never saw myself on City Council, but there I was serving on City Council. I never saw myself as a community organizer, but there I was organizing for WBQP-TV. I never imagined I could convince a majority of the people in a community to vote for me, but there I was knocking on doors and asking for votes. In the final analysis, we have more inside of us than we realize. No one person comes with all the answers, but as we journey, it's about using the tools God has already planted in your arsenal.

Looking back, I can see now how life had a strange way of taking two very different events and making their paths cross for a greater purpose. Sometimes it's just enough to spark your interest and impact those who are traveling along the path with you. In most instances it takes time to understand the meaningful connection between unrelated events. These events, however different, propelled me into a place of enlightenment that was unexpected, and yet, very exciting.

Debra A. K. Thompson

Part VII

New Home, New Life

It's funny how you can have one thing in your mind about the future and your mate can have another. Marcell and I moved to the Pensacola, Florida area in 1982 and we both found it to be a friendly and progressive city with historic appeal. I thought once we started our family, we would live in Pensacola at least until we retired and then do some traveling.

Marcell, on the other hand, liked Pensacola but he always had a desire to move the family back to the Tampa Bay area of Florida well before we reached retirement age. He never pushed really hard to make it happen, but just enough to let me know he was seriously contemplating the idea. In my mind I thought we had found a good place to settle and I saw nothing but positive things happening in our future. He saw all the good things I saw, but his long range vision was different from mine.

As I think back over the time, Marcell and I were both able to obtain decent jobs when we first moved to town. We were able to purchase a nice house in a great neighborhood with highly-rated schools and convenient shopping areas nearby. Additionally, we attended a great church and we worked diligently in various community organizations. Consequently, I saw no reason to make drastic changes in our living situation.

I never understood his desire to leave a place where our family seemed to be blossoming. Yet, he would periodically bring up the topic of moving. I am not sure why Marcell became so fixed on the idea, but it seemed to be important to him, so I had to take him seriously.

Whenever Marcell brought up the subject of moving I would say, "Why do you want to go back to St. Petersburg?"

He would respond, "I want you to be closer to your family if anything ever happens to me."

I would then ask him, "What do you think is going to happen to you?"

He would reply, "I don't expect anything to happen, but you never know. I am concerned because you can't drive, and you can't depend on friends for your transportation needs."

He was correct in the fact that I could not drive a car, but I saw this as less of a problem than he did. I don't think I ever solely relied on my friends for my transportation needs. Furthermore, I don't think I ever depended on any specific mode of transportation to meet my daily obligations. I was able to utilize several options at my disposal such as the local transit system, cabs, friends, walking, and any other means available to get where I needed to go.

Although I did not completely agree with his logic on the matter; I guess I understood what he was trying to say. I thought his concern was unwarranted. I was deeply touched because I knew this was his way of letting me know he cared.

I know the fact that I couldn't drive was more of a problem for Marcell than it was for me. I would tell him, "You don't need to worry about me because God always takes care of me." I would also remind him that I was an adult and I was perfectly capable of taking care of myself.

He would agree that I was an adult, but he would also say that he had an obligation to look out for me, too. He would sometimes say, "I took you away from your hometown and family; now I have to get you back." I can't ever remember telling him I was homesick or I wanted to move back to my hometown. I just think this was something he had in his mind and it didn't matter whether or not I agreed.

It was hard for me to get excited about a move I didn't want to make. I understood his desire to move closer to the family. We always maintained regular and consistent contact with our family, so I didn't understand his persistence. We saw the family at least three times a year and we spoke every week on the phone. However, he said his concern was not for the present, but he was trying to prepare for the future. He thought he needed to be ahead of the curve in case something ever happened to him.

I don't know what he expected to happen, and I realize anything could have happened, but in my opinion there was no need to create a problem where none existed. Yet, nothing I said seemed to change his mind. I would often remind him that if I needed to return to St. Petersburg one day, I'd know what to do when the time was right. However, it didn't seem to matter what I said or what I did, he remained firm in his position. I thought his concern for me was very touching, but his persistence on the subject was also very frustrating for me as well. I saw no reason for him to feel the way he did; consequently, I thought the best thing I could do was ignore his statements on the matter.

The first time Marcell broached the idea about leaving Pensacola was when our oldest son, Daniel was in ninth grade. His job was closing their office in Pensacola and they were relocating to the Washington, D.C. area. By this time, we had lived in Pensacola for approximately 16 years. Our son Daniel was so close to graduation I thought a move might have a negative impact on him. As a matter of fact, both Daniel and Caleb were doing so well in school I was hesitant about changing anything.

I tried to convince Marcell he should take the job in D. C. and allow me and the boys to stay in Pensacola until Daniel graduated. He wouldn't agree to this arrangement. He didn't want to leave me alone with two teenaged boys. Against my sincere urging, he turned the job down and opted to remain with us.

The second time Marcell brought up the subject of moving from Pensacola was when I was serving my first term on the Pensacola City Council. Marcell received a job offer in Tampa at MacDill Air Force Base. Just like the last time, I had no problem with him leaving us to take the job offer. However, I wasn't willing to leave Pensacola because I thought the timing wasn't right.

I did not want to resign before my term on the Council was complete. I felt the people had voted for me to do a job and I wasn't willing to let them down by resigning. Additionally, our family was so entrenched in the community that people did not even realize we were not native Pensacolians, but transplants from another area of the state.
I know it sounds kind of vain, but I enjoyed this designation very much and I didn't want to give that up. It wasn't because I didn't want to go with him, but I thought my reasons for staying were just as important.

Although I tried diligently to convince him to take the job offer in Tampa, Marcell turned the offer down. He wasn't willing to go if I wasn't willing to go with him. I felt guilty because he was missing opportunities for advancement when he turned down this position, as well as the other position in Washington, DC.

I had given him permission to leave and take advantage of his career opportunities and allow me to join him later. I know his refusal to leave stemmed from his concern for me and the children, but I truly did not understand his willingness to leave everything we had established behind to start all over again in a new place.

Although I didn't verbalize my thoughts on this subject very often, I felt in my sub-conscious mind we would eventually move to another house, but my thinking was not in-line with leaving Pensacola. My thinking was that we would find another house, but in a different area of the community. I knew Pensacola had been such a positive place for our family that I couldn't imagine living anywhere else; at least not at that time. I've had to go back and reflect on the entire period of time to grasp the lesson I now know God wanted me to learn.

As I look back, I can see now what I couldn't see then. Things were going very well for me and the family. Our children were doing well and continuing to grow up right in front of our eyes. Both Marcell and I kept busy participating in the activities with the boys. We volunteered with the band boosters, chorus, basketball, PTA, and any other related activities our children wanted to do.

Marcell played an integral part in our sons' lives. It would have been a lot more difficult for me to do all the things we accomplished together for them without him. We kept ourselves so busy, I didn't have a lot of time to think about making unnecessary changes.

Our children had the opportunity to attend great schools and excel. The boys were growing so fast. It was all we could do to keep up and have them ready to move on to college when the time was right. We had also made some great friends, both professionally and socially. I saw no reason for us to start over in another city where we had no real connections.

Not only were we busy with the children, but I was busy serving my term on the Pensacola City Council. I was also working with the grassroots organization, Movement for Change, as well as Independence for the Blind. In addition, I was the founder and coordinator of the Gospel Songwriters Music Workshop. This workshop was an integral part of my music ministry, which I loved.

Marcell also served on several community boards and associations, so I never thought about making changes to what seemed to be a wonderful life. I was very satisfied with the house we lived in and I enjoyed the neighborhood. I know we had family ties in St. Petersburg, but we hadn't lived there since 1979 and we would have to start all over building a new life in a new place if we moved.

However, in the back of my mind, a strange thought about a new house kept invading my thinking. There were times I would think about a new house, but it was just something to think about. Maybe Marcell had planted a subliminal thought in my head about moving and that's why I kept having the feeling I would get a new house eventually. I had no conscious desire to move. I didn't think too seriously or too hard about it at the time, but little things would happen that would bring the idea of moving back to the forefront of my mind.

On several occasions I would broach the subject about another house with Marcell, but he would only respond with, "We already have a house, Taffnee. Who are you going to be married to when you get this new house? If you get another house, it won't be with me. I am sure I won't be here anyway by the time you get another house."

"I'm going to be married to you. Where do you think you are going?"

He would then tease me and say, "It won't be me. You can leave that to your next husband."

"The only husband I see in front of me is you, so you better get ready." I would laugh, but I was very serious. I know he recognized that moving to another city entailed finding a new place to live, but he insisted we wouldn't get another house. I think that's why I wasn't in favor of leaving Pensacola – because I wasn't willing to give up everything we had built just to start over.

Although I couldn't imagine living anywhere else, I am just like most women who can become very excited if given an opportunity to move to a different location, especially if it involves purchasing a newer house. I knew in the back of my mind if we moved to another city we would probably purchase another house, but that was too overwhelming for me to think about at the time.

I don't know if Marcell even thought that far ahead, unless he had some kind of premonition, that eventually we would need to move closer to our family. Maybe that's why he kept bringing the subject up. I don't think he was sure when or how it would happen, and that's why he couldn't let go of the idea. Whatever the reason, he just couldn't let it go.

As time has a way of doing, it moves on. Both of our children were now out of the house and working on building independent lives of their own. We had what is commonly referred to as the proverbial "Empty Nest Syndrome" going on. By this time, I had completed my stint on City Council and had become more involved in community activism. I thought we were getting ready to travel and do all the things we both had talked about doing so frequently during the early years.

Marcell was at the point in his work career he could retire at any time if he wanted to. He would always say, "I'm ready to retire, but I've got to get this boy out of college," referring to our youngest son Caleb.

I would remind him, "You don't have to wait to retire if that's what you want to do." Being the practical man he has always been, I figured he would wait to retire when Caleb graduated from college. He was always financially astute and I knew he would make the right decision for our family, so I didn't have to worry.

However, on this particular day, Marcell came home and said he wanted to talk with me about something important after dinner. I felt a little disconcerted and confused at this request. Not because he asked to talk to me, but the look on his face and the concern in his eyes let me know it was serious. We always had pretty open communication, but his tone made me feel uneasy.

Once we finished dinner, I was anxious to find out what was going on. Marcell, what is wrong?" He didn't immediately answer my question, but he motioned for me to move back towards the kitchen table and have a seat. I had just finished the dishes from our evening meal, so I quickly hung the dish towel in its proper place and stored my apron in the drawer. As I took my seat, he looked straight into my face and eyes.

He started to speak in a quiet and deliberate manner. "Taffnee, I know our lives haven't gone the way you probably envisioned it at the beginning, but now that the children are gone, I think it's time for us to start thinking about what we are going to do from here." As he was speaking my mind was rapidly racing and my heart was pounding. I was trying to figure out where he was going with this conversation. I couldn't imagine what would be so serious that he needed my undivided attention. So I did what every rational person does at this point…I started thinking the worst.

"Alright," I thought, "suppose he is getting ready to tell me he is sick with some terminal illness that I know nothing about and he only has a short time to live. Oh my God, how could I not know something like this? No, no, no…" I went on inside my head, "Maybe he's getting ready to ask me for a divorce. I know that's got to be it! He's probably ready to call it quits after only 34 years of marriage. I knew it! He's probably tired of me with all my nagging and complaining."

The thoughts just kept running through my mind. "He's going to tell me he has lost his job! I bet he lost that good job after all these years. How could he do this to me? How could he do this to us? I know he has had some frustrations about how far he has to drive every day to work, but that's no reason to lose a good job."

It wasn't easy, but I had to bring my mind back to the present so I could hear and digest the words he was saying to me: "I've got another job offer in Tampa at MacDill Air Force Base. I know that you know I have wanted to move back to the Tampa Bay area for many years. I think it's time for us to move back closer to the family. Our children are no longer here in Pensacola and there is no reason we can't leave. Would you be willing to go?" he asked solemnly.

I was shocked and speechless. I didn't know what to say. This was so out of left-field and not at all what I expected to hear. I knew he had turned down a couple of job offers in the past because I wasn't willing to uproot the children during that time.

I continued to listen. He further explained that he knew how much I loved my "home" in Pensacola and how entrenched I was in the community. In addition, he said that he understood this was the place our children were born and raised and this was the place we had grown to love and call home for almost 30 years. "I know this won't be an easy decision, Taffnee, but I'll abide by whatever you decide."

It took me a few minutes to get myself back together before I could even respond to what he was saying. "Whoa!" I thought, "Where did this come from?" I had no idea he was considering another job offer. This conversation wasn't anything like I had imagined in my mind. "Why now?" I thought. "He's almost ready to retire in just a few more years. What is this all about?"

It was true our sons had moved away from Pensacola and both of our families lived in South Florida. Even acknowledging that, I had not given any serious thought to leaving the Pensacola area. This request was so far out; I barely knew how to respond. Moving was the last thing on my mind, so I had to regroup before I could ask my first question.

Once I composed myself, I finally asked, "When do you have to give your answer about the job, Marcell?"

"I have to let them know something by Monday. If I take the job, I'll need to be in Tampa by the end of March."

"March!" I repeated. "This is the middle of January. I don't know if I'll have time to get everything done. This is so sudden!" My head was swirling around with each word he had spoken. It almost sounded as though he was speaking a foreign language. "You mean you have to let them know something by this coming Monday?" I reiterated, "Today is Friday and you are talking about giving them an answer in only three days." Then I asked quietly, "How long have you known about this job offer?"

"I just got the offer about two weeks ago and I have a week to let them know something definite. I wasn't sure you would be willing to go so that's why I hesitated to tell you before this."

As he spoke I could tell he felt unsure about my response. I started reflecting back on all the great times and memories we had in Pensacola. I thought about the beautiful house we had purchased and the wonderful home we had made for ourselves and our family. Additionally, I reflected on all the good friends we had made during our time in the city. I loved my church, I loved working in the community, and I appreciated all the great relationships we had cultivated over the years. Consequently, I knew it wasn't going to be easy for me to make this hasty decision; but that was what I was being asked to do.

Slowly I started to get my thoughts together and, as I said a quick prayer, I began to think about all the times Marcell had sacrificed to make sure the boys and I were comfortable. He also lost out on two other job opportunities in the past because I wasn't willing to change our lives at that time. I thought things were going too well to make a hurried decision, but a decision had to be made, nonetheless. Moreover, he supported me while I was serving my term on the Pensacola City Council and did not pressure me to leave early even when it would have benefited his career.

I know Marcell saw the shock on my face and the surprise in my eyes as I tried to digest and process the information I had just heard. I felt a sense of relief because it wasn't a "terminal illness" talk, nor was it any other bad news.

My mind continued to race at a hundred miles per hour thinking of what this potential move would mean. It would mean I would be giving up the work I loved to do in the community. I would be leaving all my friends behind. I wasn't sure if I would be able to continue my Gospel Songwriters Music Workshop, or work on behalf of those who are blind and visually impaired. Just the thought of starting over was overwhelming to me.

I loved my house, my neighbors, and my neighborhood and I didn't want to leave them behind. I kept wondering if I would be able to find another home and neighborhood comparable to the one I was giving up. Also, I had just started a new radio show on WRNE and I had recently released a new CD project. As you can tell, I had lots of things on my plate. Yet, I knew I could not deny my husband this opportunity he so desperately wanted to take. I think fear of the unknown can stop you from moving forward even if the move forward is a good move.

As I sat looking at him, I could only think how hard it must have been for him to make such a request knowing all the things I was doing and the impact it would have on my life. I knew it must have been very important to him, or he would not have been contemplating such a decision. Moreover, I began to understand how difficult it was for him – always making sacrifices for me and the children. I started thinking more about him rather than myself.

It struck me right then how selfish I had been. I thought I had been doing things for the good of our family, but the truth is, it was all about what I wanted. Yes, I wanted him to be happy, but in my mind our happiness took a back seat to the happiness and well-being of the children...along with anything else I was doing.

We sat there quietly for a few minutes, then I said, "The children are now adults. I think it's about time for you to do something you want to do. You have made many career decisions trying to keep me and the boys satisfied while leaving yourself unfulfilled. Now it's your time."

I could see the relief on his face as I continued to speak. His countenance appeared to lift as he realized I was saying "yes" for the first time. It was then I understood he wasn't thinking about himself at all. As usual, he was still thinking more about me. It was hard to admit, but I was really the selfish one.

He knew both of our sons lived in South Florida and it would be good to be closer to them. He also knew my parents could use our help with other family members who had become ill and incapacitated. The bottom line was: I had no real reason why I could not go with him if he wanted to take the job in Tampa. I felt joy, sorrow, relief, and sadness all at the same time because I knew I would be closing this chapter of my life and starting a new one. The question became: could I do it in such a short period of time?

The gravity of the question he asked me started to hit me all at once. I asked again, "How much time do we *really* have before you have to give an answer?"

"We have until Monday."

As you can imagine the panic really set in! I then asked him, "How much time do we have to find a new place to live?"

He said, "We have about a month and a half.

"Oh my God!" I thought. "That only gives me a month and a half to uproot 28 years of living in one house. How in the world will we ever be able to find another suitable place to live in that amount of time?"

In my mind, this was going to be an almost impossible task, but I knew it had to be done. The thought of trying to pack up a four-bedroom house was almost too overwhelming to think about. Even though our oldest son was married with his own family and our youngest son was off in college, I still had games, toys, and clothing in their rooms. I had things I know I should have gotten rid of years ago, but somehow they had sentimental value to me so I never removed them. The old saying is really true, "You don't know how much junk you have until you have to move it."

Where would I start? How was I going to be able to pull it all together in the amount of time I was being given? What would I do first? There was so much stuff to go through. I started thinking about all the holiday decorations and the school supplies I had stashed away, all the clothing and shoes I never wore, all the old dishes and kitchen supplies, all the papers that needed shredding... There was a lot to do and so little time to do it in. I felt like saying, "Just leave it all behind and let's start over," but I knew there were some things we had to sort through in order to get rid of things we no longer needed and pack the things we needed to keep.

I finally brought my thoughts back to the present. Once I told him I would go to Tampa, it seemed like the race was on. I closed my eyes and started thinking about the things I could possibly get rid of and all the things I wanted to keep. Hard decisions would have to be made, because we did not even have a place to move whatever we decided to take.

Just then, another thought occurred to me: "Where will we live? Can we even find a place comparable to the place we have in Pensacola for a reasonable price? How will we manage to find a place and get everything packed at the same time?" It was almost too overwhelming to think about.

The next thing I thought about was, how I would tell my pastor and church members I was leaving. I had served and worshipped with them for at least 28 years and they were my spiritual family. How would I let all my friends and neighbors know we were leaving town as well? We had lived in the same house for over 25 years and everyone knew us.

I volunteered a couple of days a week at the Movement for Change Office and I served on the board of Independence for the Blind as well. I would be severing all the day-to-day ties I had come to know and love.

Although this was not easy, I came to understand this whole chapter of my life was not about me and what I wanted, but it was a lesson to teach me how to care about the desires and needs of my husband. I really thought I had been doing just that, but I finally figured out I was only concerned about myself.

I realized I would miss my friends in Pensacola, but I know my real friends would stay in contact with me even though the distance would be great. I came to the conclusion that, as a community worker, I could find rewarding work no matter where I lived.

Additionally, I loved working in the church and I could find another church as well. I knew I could never stop working with the Gospel Songwriters Music Workshop because it is my heart and my calling and it's something I could do anywhere.

The truth is that times may change and people may change, but "Home is where the heart is." I now understood that change was a natural part of life that helps us move to the next level. I finally realized that, as long as I had Marcell, my family, and a few good friends, I had everything I needed and more in order to excel no matter where I lived.

Once the light bulb came on in my mind and spirit, it became easier for me to do the things I needed to do to prepare for the move. I even became very, very excited about the relocation and the possibility of finding a new place to live. What made it even better is that Marcell said we could find another house comparable to the one we had in Pensacola.

I asked if we could look at some new homes and he agreed we could. Wow! That was very exciting to think about…a new house. It's amazing how God gives us the desires of our heart even when we don't realize He is working on our behalf. Somehow He orchestrates our life events to bring us right where we need to be at the right time…me with the new house and Marcell back home in Tampa Bay.

When Marcell said we could look for another house in Tampa Bay that would accommodate our current needs, I was happy. I loved my home town, but I had never been that excited about moving back until we started house hunting in the Tampa Bay area. Although I had so much going for me in Pensacola, somehow the changes in the landscape and the progressive development in the area only added to my excitement about moving.

I had so many new areas to choose from my enthusiasm soared. Subsequently, we were able to find another beautiful house in the Tampa Bay area that accommodated everything we needed, but with a few additions I had always wanted. My new house came with all the things we had in our house in Pensacola and more. God knows how to answer our prayers and teach us a lesson at the same time.

Of course, you know I had to remind Marcell about his attitude in the past whenever I tried to talk about moving. I always used my best Marcell imitation while reciting his response: "Who are you going to be married to when you get this new house? We already have a house. If you get another house, it won't be with me. You can leave that to your next husband. I am sure I won't be here anyway by the time you get another house."

Guess what? Now I think I get the last laugh because I tell him, "I'm still married to you and I thank God for this new house. I'm so glad you haven't gone anywhere." All Marcell can do is shake his head and eat his "barbecued crow." Somehow God knows just what to do to make everything work in our favor even if it takes a while to get there.

ENLIGHTENMENT

PART VIII

Conclusion

Enlightenment is all about growth. Looking back over the accountings of your life can help you more clearly see the growth you have attained. Taffnee learned six very valuable things through her journey which included: love, trust, appreciation, respect, patience, and forgiveness. These are all attributes many of us strive to achieve throughout our lives and yet we continue to struggle to maintain the application of each lesson. These things in and of themselves are valuable if we learn to recognize them for what they are.

Usually every lesson encompasses some aspect of love, trust, appreciation, respect, patience, and forgiveness which must be learned before proceeding to the next lesson. The take-away of any lesson is always positive – regardless of how the lesson feels as you are going through it. Sometimes it is not easy to see the positive through the eyes of a negative experience, but as you reflect back and begin to put all the pieces together, the whole is easier to recognize and understand.

If Taffnee had only reflected on the negative aspects of each lesson, then the only thing she would have received from the lessons would have been anger, bitterness, confusion, mistrust, etc. The purpose of the lesson would be lost.

Just like we must pan through dirt, sand, rock, and other sediment to find gold, it is the hard, stubborn rocks of our lives we must sort through to get to the gem stones we seek. Some people can find their gem stones of life more easily than others because they are more perceptive. It doesn't mean they are necessarily smarter or better, but it simply means different gem stones take different amounts of pressure to materialize. Some precious stones are found lying on top of the ground while other stones must be mined.

Although it may take one person longer to find their gem stones, it does not mean they are not there. It does mean more work has to be applied to find them. If you are still holding on to the negative aspects of any lesson, it means it has not been fully grasped and understood. Another lesson must be experienced in order to complete the course. That's why lessons are continually repeated until the meaning is fully realized.

Maybe you are like Taffnee, unable to recognize the value in each lesson as it happens. But as you look back, it helps on the journey forward. It may take many years and many lessons to finally get to a place of understanding some things that need to be learned, but eventually we get there. You may never understand every crack and crevice you go through, but you should be able to look back and recognize some growth.

If we continue to circle the same mountain and travel through the same valley, then there is something we are missing which must be understood if we are to ever move forward. It always seems easier to recognize the failings and shortcomings of another before we can see it in ourselves, but we must recognize and accept our own truth before we can clearly understand the specific lesson God wants to teach us.

Love is something we must constantly learn how to do. Love for ourselves, our families, and others is not always easy to maintain, especially when people are not being very lovable.

Trust is a word that is easy to say, but more difficult to practice when that trust is challenged or broken.

Appreciation is being grateful for the things you have instead of the things you want. It is being thankful for what you do have and not always worrying about the things you don't have.

Respect is caring for oneself and for others. Proper respect keeps you grounded and humble.

Patience is something we all struggle to maintain in our everyday lives. It is the attribute we are most in need of, but the one we exercise the least.

Forgiveness is one of those words we all know and like to use when it pertains to us, but we use it sparingly when we apply it to others. We must learn how to forgive the small as well as the large mistakes in our lives if we are to ever learn how to forgive the mistakes of others.

Most of us have experienced enlightenment in many areas of our lives and, without a doubt, there is more to come. Hopefully we will develop a keener sense of what to expect when it happens. As long as we live on this earth, our job is to keep growing and learning.

Always remain receptive and open to the possibilities enlightenment can bring. Also remember, as long as we have breath in our bodies, we haven't had our last enlightenment moment. There are higher heights and deeper depths available with each new day of life. Take the time to recognize and understand your enlightenment moments and make them work for you.

GLOSSARY OF TERMS

Baptist Training Union (BTU) has been a part of the African-American Baptist Church since its early beginnings. It was a part of Christian education designed to instruct all church members in basic Bible beliefs, Baptist doctrine, church membership, discipline, policy, and procedures. It was traditionally held in most Baptist Churches on Sunday evenings, prior to evening worship. It began as a training ground for young people.

Blacks in Government (BIG) was established in 1975 and incorporated in 1976 by a small group of African-Americans at the Public Health Services Office, which is a part of the Department of Health, Education, and Welfare, in the Parklawn building in Rockville, Maryland. Initially, it was thought that the umbrella organization would address only the problems at the Federal level. However, it was soon determined that State, County, and Municipal Black employees were faced with the same general type of employment problems, so the organization expanded to include all levels of government service. BIG has organized around issues of mutual concern for equality, opportunity, and fairness in the workplace. They use their collective strength to confront and resolve these issues.

Defining Moment – A moment in which an experience happens that will have an impact on your life. It is generally something which has a major impact and has the potential of changing your life course.

Discrimination - The unjust or prejudicial treatment of different categories of people or things, especially on the grounds of race, age, or sex. Prejudice, bias, bigotry, intolerance, narrow-mindedness, unfairness, inequity, favoritism, one-sidedness, or partisanship.

Enlightenment – The act of being enlightened. Pure and unqualified knowledge. Awareness and understanding.

Enlightenment Moment – A point at which another incident occurs that helps you to understand the significance of another earlier experience.

Federal Communications Commission (FCC) was established on June 19, 1934, to replace the outdated Federal Radio Commission. As communications expanded and television became more prominent, the FCC's duties were expanded to include regulating all forms of communication in the United States. The FCC helps to regulate content, award station charters, and monitor innovation to make sure that all forms of communication can co-exist. The FCC is also involved in regulating the Internet in the United States, and it has created regulations that have become the center of debate for the telecommunications industry, corporate users, and the millions of people in the United States who utilize the Internet every day.

Gospel Songwriters Music Workshop (GSMW) was established in 1994 with just a handful of participants. It started as a one-day event which culminated with a concert on the next day. It has expanded to a three-day festival with attendees from various areas of the Country.

Independence for the Blind of West Florida (IB West) – The purpose of the organization is to train and help educate those who are blind and visually impaired with technology and life skills to enhance employment opportunities. On October 1, 1995, the corporation became a self-governing, private, not-for-profit entity fully incorporated under the name of Independence for the Blind of West Florida.

Movement for Change (MFC) is a grassroots organization officially founded in October 1997 and evolved from the grassroots efforts of an organization named Progressive Alliance Community Equity Resources and Strategies (PACERS) and a committee that was formed to address renaming a Pensacola, Florida street in honor of Dr. Martin Luther King Jr., as well as additional community issues regarding the rigid, defiant attitudes of city officials.

<u>National Association for the Advancement of Colored People (NAACP)</u> - Founded on February 12. 1909, the NAACP is the nation's oldest, largest, and most widely-recognized grassroots-based civil rights organization. Its more than half-million members and supporters throughout the United States and the world are the premier advocates for civil rights in their communities, campaigning for equal opportunity and conducting voter mobilization.

<u>National Black Child Development Institute (NBCDI)</u> - The organization was launched by the Black Women's Community Development Foundation, whose leadership in the wake of the Civil Rights Movement was deeply concerned about the unsatisfactory conditions faced by families determined to raise healthy Black children. NBCDI's focus has been on achieving positive outcomes for vulnerable children who suffer from the dual legacies of poverty and racial discrimination.

<u>Prejudice</u> - Preconceived opinion that is not based on reason or actual experience. Preconception, prejudgment. Dislike, hostility, or unjust behavior deriving from unfounded opinions.

<u>Southern Christian Leadership conference (SCLC)</u> - The very beginnings of the SCLC can be traced back to the Montgomery Bus Boycott. The Montgomery Bus Boycott began on December 5, 1955 after Rosa Parks was arrested for refusing to give up her seat to a White man. The boycott lasted for 381 days and ended on December 21, 1956. The boycott was carried out by the Montgomery Improvement Association (MIA.) Martin Luther King, Jr. served as President and Ralph David Abernathy served as Program Director. After the boycott, 60 persons from ten states, along with the MIA leadership, assembled and announced the founding of the Southern Leadership Conference on Transportation and Nonviolent Integration. It was open to all, regardless of race, religion, or background.

WBQP TV is a local low-power television station in Pensacola, Florida founded by Vernon and Mary Lynn Watson. The station was organized to provide programming with the African-American Community in mind. The FCC issued the call sign W12CN and licensed them to broadcast on channel 12 in Pensacola in June of 1992. The State of Florida assigned a d.b.a. (doing business as) to Watson Broadcasting of Pensacola and WBOP was created. Vernon & Mary Lynn Watson became the first African-Americans in Pensacola, Florida to own a broadcast television station. The station was later renamed WBQP in 1995.

White Flight – The movement of White city-dwellers to the suburbs to escape the influx of minorities. "White flight" is a term that originated in the United States, starting in the mid-20th century, and applied to the large-scale migration of Whites of various European ancestries from racially-mixed urban regions to more racially-homogeneous suburban or ex-urban regions.

Acknowledgements

This book has been a labor of love for me, but I couldn't have done it without some very special people lending me a helping hand to get the work done. Abundant thanks to my dear friend and sister, Etheldra Sharpe. Etheldra spent many long nights with me reading, re-reading, and editing this book. Only a dear friend like her would spend so many sleepless nights working with me and encouraging me to move forward. Also many thanks go out to my dear friends Marilyn Mills, Ellis Jones, and Diane Bibb Williams, who took the time to read my manuscript and provide endless amounts of insightful help to make this book the best it could possibly be. The suggestions and comments they provided helped me improve my work tremendously.

Thanks to my mom and dad who always gave me unconditional love. I don't think anyone could have been raised by any better parents than I had. Additionally, I am very fortunate to have sisters who support me no matter what venture I undertake, they are always there.

Finally, thanks to my dear friends Mary Armstrong and Amanda Richardson for being supportive and always there when I need them. Couldn't have done it without both of these ladies.

About The Author

Debra A. K. Thompson is a freelance writer who lives in Riverview, Florida with her husband. She currently writes short stories and articles for a local magazine called *The Church Bulletin.* Debra has also written numerous specialty articles for *Flavor Magazine,* as well as feature articles for a popular Christian magazine, *The Gospel Express.* She is a prolific songwriter who founded and continues to coordinate the Gospel Songwriters Music Workshop, which is an annual conference for aspiring and veteran songwriters.

Debra obtained her Bachelor's Degree from the University of South Florida and a Master's Degree from Florida State University. She served one term on the Pensacola City Council and she was appointed to the Florida Rehabilitation Council by Governor Jeb Bush.

Debra A. K. Thompson

www.ingramcontent.com/pod-product-compliance
Lightning Source LLC
Chambersburg PA
CBHW052006090426
42741CB00008B/1570